THE DRUG, THE SOUL, AND GOD

A THEOLOGICAL PERSPECTIVE
ON
ANTIDEPRESSANTS

THE DRUG, THE SOUL, AND GOD

A THEOLOGICAL PERSPECTIVE
ON
ANTIDEPRESSANTS

John-Mark L. Miravalle

University of Scranton Press
Scranton and London

Library of Congress Cataloging-in-Publication Data

Miravalle, John-Mark L., 1982-
  The drug, the soul, and God : a theological perspective on antidepressants /
John-Mark L. Miravalle.
    p. cm.
  Includes bibliographical references.
  ISBN 978-1-58966-192-9 (pbk.)
  1. Antidepressants--Religious aspects--Catholic Church. 2. Depression, Mental-
-Religious aspects--Catholic Church. I. Title.
  RM332.M545 2009
  615'.78--dc22

                                                          2009049130

Distribution:

University of Scranton Press
Chicago Distribution Center
11030 S. Langley
Chicago, IL 60628

For Jessica

CONTENTS

INTRODUCTION

Nearly everyone is aware of the prevalence of antidepressant use. Most Americans have personal acquaintance with someone who is taking one of the many common prescription drugs to combat depression. As Carl Elliot notes, "the notion of 'clinical depression' has expanded tremendously to include many people who might once have been called melancholy, anxious, or alienated,"[1] so it does not appear that these prescriptions will lessen dramatically in the near-future.

Yet the ubiquity of the drugs has caused a good deal of public discomfort and has even occasioned condemnation. Many are alarmed by the idea of using a pill as a solution to mental problems. Such a therapy seems somehow dehumanizing, and perhaps mechanistic. There appears to be something intuitively unsettling about the notion that unhappy patients can be relieved of their unhappiness through the efficacy of a pharmaceutical agent, but the volume of prescriptions continues to increase nevertheless. In a culture so influenced by these medications, it is important that these criticisms be either vindicated or dismissed, and that proper guidelines be formulated that stipulate when the prescription of these drugs is justifiable and when it is morally objectionable.

Unfortunately, concerns about antidepressant usage are frequently expressed in vague terms, such that often the only thing conveyed is a sense of uneasiness about how and when to use the drugs. Normally, the arguments advanced regarding what constitutes acceptable antidepressant usage are rather less than conclusive. A likely reason for this inability to convey exactly what is wrong with indiscriminately issued antidepressant prescriptions is that modern psychiatry appears to lack a uniform and well-defined anthropology.[2] What is the human person? How is one to care for him? What constitutes human wellness? Without clear answers to these questions, professionals may be deprived of the basis of authentic psychology and morality (both sciences depending on an accurate anthropological model) for forming guidelines for the proper distribution of mood-altering drugs.

I propose that the Catholic moral tradition can offer the necessary anthropological standard; that its understanding of the human person, inclusive of the spiritual, moral, and even supernatural dimensions,[3] will provide sufficient insight for the articulation of principles governing the use of antidepressant drugs. This book considers the question of antidepressant drug prescriptions from within the framework of this tradition for the purpose of developing norms to clarify when antidepressant use is legitimate and beneficial, and when it is potentially harmful to the patient.

The first step in our study must be to examine carefully the status of depression and antidepressants in contemporary society, scientifically, culturally, and clinically. To this subject matter is devoted the first chapter. Following this, chapter II will draw upon the masterful psychological treatment of St. Thomas Aquinas in order to expound the inner structure of the emotional life and, more specifically, of sorrow and depression. The third chapter explores those principles found within the Catholic moral tradition that bear upon the question of antidepressant drugs. Primary attention will be given to the principle of integrity: its elucidation, instances of its magisterial application to particular cases (most notably that of contraception), and its protection of the basic good of inner peace. The next chapter will make use of these principles in suggesting parameters for the ethical use of antidepressant drugs, guidelines by which we may distinguish when these medications cause real damage to the individual and when they are of service. Lest the analysis give the impression of being too abstract, chapter V offers a concrete model of clinical psychiatry that successfully embodies the conclusions of the preceding chapters. Last, in addition to the naturally discernable aspects of the spiritual and moral spheres, Catholicism is graced with knowledge of man's supernatural destiny, and the providential plan for his heavenly fulfillment. The sixth chapter addresses how the enlightenment of faith affects the Christian's proper attitude toward suffering, which in turn has ramifications respecting the dangers of antidepressant misuse.

From the outset it is well to make several qualifications. In debates over ethical antidepressant use, much is made of the various side effects of antidepressant medications. Nonetheless, our argument will for the most part prescind from the issue of side effects, for two reasons. The first is that there is a considerable degree of debate concerning the frequency, permanence, and severity of the side affects of the various drugs in use. "People respond to antidepressants in ways that are anything but uniform."[4] To enter such a debate would take the discussion too far afield.[5]

The second and more important reason for avoiding a discursion into the nature of antidepressant side effects is that by definition side effects are the unintended byproducts of an action, and, hence, do not belong to the object of a moral action, but rather to the category of circumstances.

Provided that the side effect is not willed as either a means or an end, it is excluded from the notion of the action in and of itself. In traditional Catholic morality, this is known as the principle of "double effect." Of course, this is not to say that a medication's side effects will be irrelevant; in fact it may be that in a given case the nature of the side effects will determine whether or not a certain treatment is morally acceptable. Yet such considerations will necessarily be limited to the specifics of the individual situation, and are consequently relegated to the domain of prudence. Our goal is to discover, in principle, the norms that distinguish morally acceptable antidepressant use from antidepressant use that is morally objectionable.

Nor will these drugs be examined except in light of their use for treating depression. Antidepressants may be prescribed for those with mania, anxiety, and other disorders, but for the sake of precision, we will simply consider them in relation to those patients suffering from depression. Certainly, the principles and applications made in this treatment can, to some degree, be extended to the controversies surrounding the pharmacological treatment of diverse psychological ailments (a prime example being attention deficit disorder), but that application would have to await later developments.

I

WHAT ARE ANTIDEPRESSANTS?

Julia used to say, "Poor Sebastian. It's something chemical in him."
That was the cant phrase of the time, derived from heaven knows what misconception of popular science. "There's something chemical between them" was used to explain the overmastering hate or love of any two people. It was the old concept of determinism in a new form. I do not believe there was anything chemical in my friend.

— Evelyn Waugh, *Brideshead Revisited*

In laying the groundwork for our analysis, we must first consider the phenomenon of depression and antidepressant drugs and their increasingly pervasive role in current society. Since the discovery of antidepressants about fifty years ago, they have been the object of much attention and great demand. Depression itself has also been studied increasingly more thoroughly, as the number of people reportedly suffering from depression increases. Depression costs the United States an estimated 16 billion dollars every year, with anywhere from 3 percent to 13 percent of the population suffering from depression.[6] Stefan Klein puts it concisely: "Depression is threatening to become the plague of the twenty-first century."[7] This plague of depression has provided a massive market to the drug industry, with the rate of prescriptions growing consistently.[8] Approximately one American in ten has used antidepressants.[9]

With the advent of antidepressants has come a host of new and often confused notions about the physiology of depression and the operation of antidepressant drugs. This section will provide a brief introduction to depression and antidepressants, explore the thesis that depression is a biochemical imbalance, and show the limits of current antidepressant science.

Before continuing, however, we wish to forestall any possible misunderstanding by stating that our intention is not to condemn any or all forms of palliative treatment, that is, treatment that is primarily geared towards the reduction of pain and/or other symptoms. Rather our purpose is simply to show that, so far as the current evidence suggests, antidepressant medications are, in fact palliative, and not curative; they do not address the root of the disorder.[10] The implications of this fact will then be drawn out in later chapters.

The Phenomenon of Depression

The American Medical Association (AMA) defines depression (also called "major depression," "major depressive disorder" or "clinical depression") as a state in which a person's unhappy feelings "become inappropriate, extreme, and dysfunctional . . . an overwhelming and debilitating despondency that is long lasting and typically interferes with a person's life at home, in the workplace, or in social situations."[11] What fundamentally distinguishes depression from ordinary sadness is its severity and duration, which are deemed excessive, as well as its compromising effect on various aspects of the individual's life and productivity.

More specific definitions indicate various forms, or categories, of depression. Major depressive disorder is the most widespread form and is characterized chiefly by extended sadness and/or a loss of pleasure in former sources of enjoyment. Those suffering from major depressive disorder may also experience self-loathing, changes in eating habits, sleep disturbances, and thoughts of suicide. Variations of this disorder include psychotic depression (identified by the presence of delusions or hallucinations), atypical depression (in which the person displays some symptoms that rarely accompany depression), postpartum depression (a condition affecting some women shortly after giving birth), and premenstrual dysphoric disorder (depression and/or irritability affecting some women before or during menstruation in which "symptoms are much more severe than those associated with premenstrual syndrome").[12]

Dysthymia, also called minor depression, is a state of gloominess in which the symptoms are not as severe as major depression. However, a diagnosis of dysthymia is normally reserved for those who have endured this unhappy state for two years or more. Seasonal affective disorder (SAD) is a depressive condition associated with seasonal changes. Individuals suffering from bipolar depression (also called bipolar disorder, manic depression, or manic-depressive illness) alternate between depression (extreme unhappiness) and mania (extreme euphoria), with both poles often leading to erratic behavior.[13]

Regarding the causes of depression, the traditional understanding conceives it as being based upon personal thoughts and experiences. Those who still ascribe to this model will naturally advise that the fundamental mode of treatment be some form of psychotherapy.[14] The most common psychotherapies for depression are currently psychoanalysis/psychodynamic therapy (which seeks to explore the patient's past and subconscious), cognitive therapy (which seeks to correct unhealthy thought patterns), and behavior therapy, also called behavior modification therapy (which uses a reinforcement/punishment technique for curing problematic behaviors). Other psychotherapies are also available.[15]

On the other hand, in the last half-century, depression has been increasingly viewed as the result of a physiological illness. Neurotransmitter activity in the brain, hormonal levels, sleep patterns, body rhythms, genes, as well as other biological causes have all been suggested as the foundation for depression.[16] Individuals who view depression as an ailment of the body will probably recommend as a primary form of treatment some direct material intervention.[17] Although physiological theories of depression have existed since ancient times,[18] the emergence of antidepressant medications has had a marked effect on the way in which depression is viewed by the psychiatric community in general. These treatments have "resulted in renewed claims that depression is biological and caused by biochemical imbalances."[19] Consequently, we will now turn our attention to antidepressant medications, their discovery and development, the various theories of their agency, and their effect upon the common understanding and treatment of depression.

Brief History of Antidepressant Development

In 1952, the wonder-drug *chlorpromazine* was discovered, initiating the revolution of psychopharmacology.[20] Chlorpromazine was first tested on mice, and had the interesting effect of making the mice unwilling to perform the tasks necessary for obtaining food. The drug was then given to asylum patients suffering from psychosis, with extremely powerful results: many patients' hallucinations and delusions subsided. The enthusiasm over chlorpromazine led to intensive research for developing drugs with a similar molecular structure. This structure is characterized by three central rings, and is hence referred to as "tricyclic." One of these experimental tricyclic drugs (G22355 or imipramine) was found to have antidepressant properties. Roland Kuhn, who had reportedly discovered this feature of imipramine, set about promoting the drug and its properties in 1956. Imipramine and its tricyclic descendents were the antidepressant drugs until the selective serotonin reuptake inhibitors (SSRIs) gained priority several decades later.

More or less simultaneously with the advent of tricyclics came the development of another form of antidepressant drugs, the MAOIs (or monoamine oxidase inhibitors). After the discovery of an enzyme that worked by oxidizing the excess of certain chemicals critical to brain functioning (monoamine oxidase), Al Zeller discovered in 1952 that iproniazid counteracted this process of oxidation, thus qualifying as a monoamine oxidase inhibitor. Four years later, Nathan Kline and his associates began experimenting with iproniazid to determine its mental effects. They declared that it, too, had antidepressant powers. Nonetheless, due to the accompanying side affects, the MAOIs were not as well received as the tricyclics for purposes of mood management.

Neither the MAOIs nor the tricyclics were predicted as antidepressants; it was only after experimentation that the drugs' unforeseen antidepressant properties were revealed. It was, by all admissions, a "chance discovery."[21] Even after this serendipitous occurrence, the internal mechanism by which the drugs were able to alter mood was not understood. "When the neuroleptics and later the antidepressants were first introduced, little or nothing was known about brain chemistry."[22] However, prompted by the excitement over the new psychiatric drugs, scientists brought brain activity to the fore of research, and it soon became apparent that the primary form of transmission in the brain occurs by means of chemical neurotransmitters (previously, it had been theorized that neuron-to-neuron communication took place via direct electrical impulses).[23]

With the isolation and identification of several neurotransmitter compounds, numerous hypotheses were suggested regarding which chemical levels were related to depression. It appeared that heightening the levels of neurotransmitters resulted in an effective treatment for depression. The MAOIs prevented certain brain chemicals from being oxidized, and it was proposed by Julius Axelrod that the tricyclic antidepressants (TCAs) prevented the reuptake of neurotransmitters, such as norepinephrine, leaving higher levels of the compound in the synapse.[24] It now seemed certain that mood could be affected by the manipulation of neurotransmitter levels. But which neurotransmitter(s) should be targeted? Which chemical was primarily responsible for the phenomenon of depression and/or its cure?

The three neurotransmitters given primary attention in the field of antidepressant research are serotonin, norepinephrine, and dopamine. These three are still referenced most frequently in popular discussion about antidepressants. "Serotonin has been shown to have the strongest association with mood regulation; norepinephrine has more influence on the brain's hormonal response; and dopamine is correlated most often with reward-mediated behavior."[25] From the mid-1960s through the 1970s, the most popular neurotransmitters associated with depression in the United States were the catecholamines, most notably norepinephrine. Serotonin (5HT), however, was a constant competitor in terms of primacy of attention, and finally gained prominence of place in the mid-1980s when the SSRIs took over the market. The SSRIs remain the most used antidepressants today, prescribed for over 34 million U.S. residents.[26] Nonetheless, the legitimacy of conceding the SSRIs this prevalence is often challenged. Indeed, claims are increasing to the effect that this trinity of chemicals is not as relevant to depression as was once thought. Stephen Braun, for instance, declares, "Not only is depression *not* caused by a lack of serotonin, norepinephrine, or dopamine . . . but also these are not the only — or even perhaps the most important — neurotransmitters related to mood."[27]

Of special relevance is the concern that throughout these various stages of research, the development of antidepressant theory was less guided by the data collected through experimentation and clinical studies than by the availability and marketability of the various drugs, as well as the many political factors within the scientific arena. Healy summarizes the situation thus:

> Far, then, from providing answers to the questions of how anti-depressants work or to the question of what is actually wrong in the nervous systems of people who are depressed, the biological investigations involved have played a different role. In essence, they have provided biological justification for the new approaches that were taken up by psychiatry during the 1970s and 1980s. They have provided artistic verisimilitude by allowing psychiatrists, who talked about biology, to appear scientific. They have provided potent images that entered popular consciousness and replaced older notions of dynamic problems. To a greater or lesser extent many of these biological notions have provided badges of identity for particular groups of individuals within the psychiatric or neuroscientific communities. People identify themselves as catecholamine persons or 5HT persons and as biologically oriented rather than socially oriented. As a sociological phenomenon, the power of such ideas in disciplines such as psychiatry to command brand-name loyalty and the re-assurance that such brand-name loyalty provides should not be underestimated. . . . [T]here is a real sense at present, then, that knowledge in psychopharmacology doesn't become knowledge unless it has a certain commercial value. The survival of concepts depends on the interests with which they coincide.[28]

Throughout the development of antidepressants, then, a great deal of progress in both drug manufacture and brain study has occurred, and yet the scientific foundation for the widespread use of antidepressants remains inconclusive. Even after it had been determined that the drugs did in fact exercise some influence on test subjects, still there was no sign that the *medicines* were in any way curative, in the sense of fixing a physiological problem. At no point in the antidepressant research was there ever any link between a clear biological defect and the phenomenon of depression. Biochemical theories of depression did and do abound, and yet as analyses such as Healy's makes clear, nothing even resembling a consensus has ever been reached. Consequently, the relentless movement to develop *better* antidepressant drugs has not been so much an effort to find the one chemical remedy to the basic problem of depression, but rather to arrive at a treatment that is most effective in its externally discernable results.

Lithium and Electroconvulsive Therapy

To illustrate the discrepancy that may exist between a treatment's curative power and its power merely to produce external effects, let us consider the cases of the antidepressants lithium and electroconvulsive therapy, or ECT. These two forms of therapy are unique in that they do not target specific neurotransmitters, and hence do not venture any claims for fixing a chemical imbalance. Lithium is a metallic substance that readily forms salt,[29] and like lead is commonly found in the human body due to its frequent presence in drinking water. Unlike the various amine levels, which are the center of attention for the MAOIs, TCAs, and SSRIs, the physiological function of lithium (if indeed any exists) is unknown. Further, the dosage used in treatment is admittedly close to various levels of toxicity.[30] Nonetheless, since it was found to have sedative properties, lithium was promoted as an appropriate treatment for depression and other various disorders. Here we may mention in passing that the effects of lithium all point to a general retardation and dulling of the patient's mental and emotional states. Side effects in lithium subjects include "poor concentration," "mental confusion," "mental slowness," "indifference," "malaise," and "the feeling of being at a distance from their environment."[31]

Regardless of the potential side effects, the fact remains that there is little indication that lithium corrects a physiological pathology. Furthermore, there does not appear to be any relation between serotonin, norepinephrine, or other neurotransmitter levels commonly associated with depression, and lithium. Nonetheless, since it proved effective in changing behavior patterns, it was considered a legitimate option in dealing with depression, and at one point it was even suggested (on an alarming scale) that lithium be added to the drinking water in the United States.[32]

Yet perhaps the most vivid example of a treatment that does not even hazard an appeal to targeting a specific cerebral disorder is the still-common practice of electroconvulsive therapy (ECT). In the United States, approximately 100,000 patients a year receive this treatment, which fundamentally consists in shocking the subject repeatedly.[33] The helpful manual, *Making the Antidepressant Decision: How to Choose the Right Treatment for You or Your Loved One* (certainly not an anti-antidepressant text) describes the process as follows:

> In modern ECT treatments, the patient is given an anesthetic and a muscle relaxant before padded electrodes are applied to one or both of the temples. A controlled electric pulse is delivered to the electrodes until the patient experiences a brain seizure; treatment usually consists of six to twelve seizures (two or three a week). After the treatment, the patient may experience a period of confusion which is later forgotten, and a brief period of amnesia covering the period of time right before the treatment. On regaining consciousness, patients who have received ECT seem much like those who have experienced post-traumatic amnesia. Tests on memory have revealed a temporary memory impairment; after a number of treatments some patients say they experience a more serious memory loss involving everyday forgetfulness, which usually disappears a few weeks after treatment. . . . All patients show some amount of amnesia for events immediately before the treatment.[34]

The *therapeutic* mechanism of ECT appears to be little more than brain damage; Max Fink states that brain dysfunction is the "*sine qua non* of the mode of action."[35] Peter Breggin points out that the relief from depression lasts around four weeks, which is the "approximate period of time during which the patient's brain dysfunction, with associated euphoria or apathy, is most severe."[36] Fundamentally, ECT consists in violently disabling the normal function of the brain in order to improve mood (or at least eliminate mood altogether to create a comfort stage of indifference).

The point is that ECT does not seem to treat a specific brain ailment associated with depression. The idea that the mechanism of shock therapy involves correcting a chemical imbalance appears untenable, and is (to the credit of the psychiatrists) not even proposed. Yet the patient's undesirable symptoms have been effectively lessened or removed; ECT treatment *works*, and the practice continues. "ECT is almost certainly the treatment that is least specific to a particular neurotransmitter system [to say the least!], but it is believed by many clinicians to be the most effective."[37] Here, then, we have a clinical treatment of depression that does not by any standard rest on the principle of solving a biochemical imbalance.[38]

Status of Scientific Efforts to Correlate Depression and a Biological Disorder

Upon further inspection, one finds scientific evidence for the very notion of depression as a chemical imbalance to be sparse. "We do not yet have proof either of the cause or the physiology for any psychiatric diagnosis."[39] In an article titled, "Mood-Mending Medicines: Probing Drug, Psychotherapy, and Placebo Solutions," researchers Seymour Fisher and Roger P. Greenberg give the following status report on the biochemical theory of depression:

> Demonstrating that affective disordered patients show quantifiable defects in brain structure or function has also proven to be problematic. Thus, despite a lot of conjecture about a biological basis for mood disorders, there is as yet no convincing consistent evidence for any biochemical theory of causation. Although this fact is often camouflaged amidst weighty scientific discussion in most textbooks, ultimately there is usually an acknowledgment of the uncertainty that is characteristic of current biological explanations.[40]

This lack of evidence is manifested by the fact that there are currently no known biological markers for effectively identifying depression. "Scientists increasingly believe that most of these psychic disorders are — like schizophrenia — partly the product of, or at least correlated with, certain underlying abnormalities and (partially heritable) disorders in the brain. Yet there are at present no specific diagnostic tests to prove the point."[41] This fact may well surprise many people familiar with the now-common conception of depression as a physiological malady, but the reality remains that the scientific community has not established or even claimed to establish a biological correlate for depression. "Despite decades of research, thousands of research studies, and hundreds of millions of dollars in expense, no marker for depression has been found."[42]

Further corroboration concerning the lack of evidence may be found in T.J. Connor and B.E. Leonard's thorough summary of all the current hypotheses concerning the neurochemical signs for depression. The authors warn at the beginning of their study that "there is a lack of integration of the various theories."[43] Connor and Leonard proceed to evaluate the numerous tests that have sought to correlate depression with some physically tangible phenomenon. Beginning with the noradrenaline and serotonin systems, and moving on to other neurotransmitters, the results are far from conclusive. Each study appearing to have located some marker for depression is quickly compared with other studies with contrary results. For example, studies by four groups conclude that CSF concentrations of the serotonin metabolite (5-HIAA) were low in depressed patients, yet four other studies "reported that there was either no change, or even an increase, in CSF 5-HIAA in depressed patients."[44] Throughout this effort to link depression and some physiological symptom, a similar pattern continues with conflicting and inconclusive results. Connor and Leonard conclude that "until the time when reliable biological markers are identified, the psychiatrist's clinical judgment remains the most valid means of diagnosing and treating depressive disorder."[45] Both doctors remain hopeful that biological markers will soon be identified. Other sources also maintain the notion of depression as biochemically caused, but admit the poverty of concrete evidence in support of such a theory.[46]

Some, however, voice dissatisfaction at the categorization of depression as a biochemical phenomenon, in the absence of conclusive evidence for such a claim:

> Biological psychiatry advocates often do not even bother to name the particular biochemical that is supposedly out of balance, or they change the allegedly offending biochemical depending on what kind of drug they are pushing. In reality, science does not have the ability to measure the levels of any biochemical in the tiny spaces between nerve cells (the synapses) in the brain of a human being. All the talk about biochemical imbalances is sheer speculation aimed at promoting psychiatric drugs.[47]

Further, not only is there no established biological sign of depression, but the modus operandi of the therapeutic drugs is far from being fully understood by the medical community. It is often unclear as to why these medical treatments actually work. W. D. Hurst summarizes the current problem:

> From relatively simple beginnings a half century ago, our attempts to describe drug influences on the brain and neuronal functions have become quite complex. Whereas we once spoke of drugs blocking neurotransmitter uptake, causing neurotransmitter release or depletion, or influencing receptors, today we understand that all of these basic neuronal processes are, in reality, complex molecular events that involve multiple control factors. *Identifying a specific molecular mechanism in a drug's action on neuronal function is, in fact, very much like a search for a needle in a haystack.* . . . As our understanding of basic neuronal and synaptic processes increases, so does the number

of potential sites or mechanisms for the expression of depressive behavior and for drug actions. The needle is still only a needle, but the haystack continues to grow larger.[48] (Italics mine).

Hence, although there are a great many theories as to why and how antidepressants work, (e.g., neurotransmitter release, reuptake, etc.), there is simply no professional consensus. "There is not widespread agreement as to how any of the antidepressants achieve their results, beyond the fact that they in various ways prolong the presence of neurotransmitters in the synapse."[49]

The fact of the matter is that there is no scientific evidence for a physiological correlation to depression, nor is there a general accord as to the agency of the antidepressants. As might be expected, this inability to link depression with a chemical imbalance, combined with a lack of clarity regarding the chief mechanism of the various drugs, manifests itself further in ordinary clinical treatment. Since doctors are in the difficult position of prescribing drugs without having any clear idea of the biology of their patients' problem, it is not surprising that the prescriptions for individual patients are themselves rather experimental. There is a large selection of considerably diverse drugs from which to pick, and any one of them might do the job: "One of the most intriguing phenomena in the pharmacological treatment of affective disorders is the availability of a wide variety of antidepressant drugs with no apparent structural relationship, but possessing similar clinical efficacies."[50] The current approach involves carefully trying to determine what works for what person; proceeding cautiously until the desired effects are manifested. One professional, Dr. Myerson, describes the situation as follows:

> It's a crapshoot. . . . We don't have good guidelines about which person will do well on which drug. So we just have to wade through, try different drugs, adjust dosages, and add drugs to drugs. You can have two patients who look identical, but one will respond well to Zoloft and one to Prozac. And we have no idea why.[51]

In the absence of both a reliable biological sign of depression and a clear understanding of how antidepressants function, many individual clinicians are working from the same principle as those who develop and market the drug, that is, external effectiveness. The main criterion can only be, they maintain, is the medications producing the desired behavioral results? Using this standard, the ideal antidepressant is the one that works best with few and minimal side effects.

The "Biochemical Imbalance" Theory

Given all this, why is the idea of depression as a biochemical phenomenon so widespread in today's culture? If a definite link between a physiological disorder and depression has never been found, how did such a model develop and diffuse itself so thoroughly into the mainstream consciousness? The answer is certainly multifaceted, and an adequate treatment of this cultural phenomenon cannot be given here. It seems rather likely that much of the misunderstanding has been caused by over-zealous campaigns of pharmaceutical companies as well as premature declarations by eager pioneer researchers. Carl Elliott discusses further how the common strategy of pharmaceutical companies is not merely to market the drug, but to market the disease:

> National Depression Awareness Day began in 1991 and is now a national media event. In October of each year, hospitals and universities around the country offer free depression screening. People are encouraged to dial twenty-four-hour 800-numbers and take an automated depression screening test. At the end of the test, a computer analyzes the score and tells the person the severity of his or her symptoms. Who pays for the press kits, the 800-numbers, and the depression screening kits? Eli Lilly, the manufacturer of Prozac.[52]

However, our interest here concerns not so much various historical occurrences as the basic fallacy that has brought about this false conviction regarding the supposed biological basis for depression. This fallacy originated at the start of the antidepressant revolution, when the discovery of TCAs and MAOIs was said to have "demonstrated that major depression was amenable to medical interventions just like other medical conditions such as hypertension or diabetes."[53] The popular antidepressant fallacy enters when one takes the premise that depression and diabetes can both be treated chemically, and goes on to conclude that the two problems must both stem from physiological bases:

> In the absence of any verifiable diseases, in recent decades, psychopharmacology has not hesitated to construct "disease models" for psychiatric diagnoses. These models are hypothetical suggestions of what *might* be the underlying physiology — for example, a serotonin imbalance. Through the 1970s and 1980s, a curious circularity invaded psychiatry, as "diseases" began to be "modeled" on the medications that "treat" them. If a drug elevated serotonin in test tubes, then it was presumptuously argued

that patients helped by the medication must have serotonin deficiencies. . . . In the past decade, as part of promoting the new antidepressants, these "disease models" were presented to patients as if they were established facts.[54]

Somehow, a great portion of the scientific community has made the logical leap from "is chemically treatable" to "is chemically based." Upon reflection such a leap reveals itself as being hard to defend. To apply this relationship between illness and treatment consistently would demand one take the premise "crutches help a man with a broken leg to walk" and go on to conclude that his problem is rooted in a lack of sufficient crutches. Crutches are geared toward one of the more inconvenient symptoms, but they do not in themselves directly address the core defect, namely, the broken leg. It seems likely that the same relationship holds between antidepressants and depression. Notice, too, that this line of argument used in supporting antidepressants could easily be applied to other drugs used for mood enhancement. As Peter Breggin accurately observes,

> However, the seeming effectiveness of a psychoactive drug by no means indicates that it is addressing an underlying medical problem. Human beings have used alcohol, coca leaves (cocaine), and a variety of herbs for thousands of years to alleviate emotional suffering, including feelings of depression or melancholy. The fact that a drug such as alcohol or cocaine can relieve sadness or other painful emotions such as anxiety or chronic anger in no way indicates that the painful emotional state has a biological origin.[55]

What is unfortunate is that the flaws in the "drugs are effective, so the problem is fundamentally biological" logic have not been more universally apparent. On the contrary, the result of this faulty reasoning has been a cultural shift in the way depression was conceived and treated. "Where once lay people had gone to psychiatrists expecting to hear about sexual repression, they now came knowing that something might be wrong with their amines or with some brain chemical."[56]

One might object here: "Very well, so there is as of yet no evidence that depression is biologically based; we have no physiological marker at this point. But soon a marker will be discovered, and the scientific community will be able to correlate depression with a tangible bodily sign, proving that depression is chemically based." The proper response to such an objection is to point out that a corresponding marker is in no way equivalent to an underlying cause. Granted the intimate relationship between the mind and body, and granted that mental states can bring about a physio-logical change and vice versa, it would still be a grave error to simply equate the two. Take for example the lie-detector. The principle behind this machine is that when a person tells an untruth, his breathing and/or heart rate are distinctly and perceptibly affected. In other words, there is a phys-iological marker for the phenomenon of lying. However, this correspon-dence could in no way justify the assertion that a certain heartbeat or breath pattern is the cause of all human lies. Joseph Glenmullen, describing the same fallacy, uses a different example:

> Even if a biochemical imbalance were found in some depressed patients, this would not necessarily mean that it was the cause of the problem. Suppose one day you were standing on a street corner waiting for the bus home when someone came along and robbed you at gunpoint. Your assailant heaps abuse and death threats upon you as he absconds with your money, jewelry, and other valuables. You are left traumatized and panicked at the thought that he will return for you. If you ran to the nearest med-ical clinic, you might well be diagnosed with a biochemical im-balance. All kinds of stress hormones and chemical signals would be coursing through your brain and body. But these bio-chemical events would be the result of your psychological dis-tress, not the cause. They would be the cart, not the horse. This would not be anything like a sodium imbalance causing behav-ioral disturbances. If a biochemical imbalance is ever found, it should come as no surprise that psychological states have phys-iological correlates.[57]

Clearly, then, a biological marker will not in and of itself be sufficient proof for the categorization of depression as a primarily biological disorder. Al-though such a marker may, if it is ever found, be helpful in the recognition of depression (say, in the case of a patient denying his problem), it will not answer the dilemma regarding the basis of depression.

So far the point here has not been to judge the moral legitimacy of antidepressant drug use but simply to dispel the widespread preconception that any conclusive evidence supporting the model of depression as a fun-damentally physiological problem exists.

Clinical Psychopharmacology in Present Practice

Despite the lack of scientific connection, the treatment of depression as a mere physiological disorder prevails. The following passage by Dr. James

Morrison might serve as a basic summary of what a depressed patient might expect to hear in a psychiatrist's office:

> I can confidently report some of the things that depression is *not*. For example, if you have depression you are not just imagining it, [nor] is it just "anger turned inward" (as Freud famously stated), nor are you merely reacting to misfortune. . . . Depression is not punishment for sin, it doesn't mean you have a weak character, and you can't "just pull yourself out of it." What's true about depression is that it isn't your fault. Depression is an illness, every bit as much as diabetes or a broken leg.[58]

Dr. Morrison, in what is doubtless an effort to comfort those suffering from depression, has essentially removed their mental problem from the sphere of their control or personal experience to the level of a broken leg. The patient may have rid himself of the pain of a felt responsibility, but he seems to have sacrificed something very human in the process. Depression has lost all personal meaning, all significance.

The biochemical model of depression is often bolstered by the common phenomenon of post-partum depression, also referred to as post-natal depression. Since in this case depression follows a biological event, one which involves great physical duress, hormonal changes, the expulsion of an autonomous organism, and so forth, the post hoc propter hoc logic claims that post-partum depression is a clear case of physiologically grounded depression. This fallacy is further compounded by a false universalization (i.e., post-partum depression is clearly a biological ailment; therefore, all forms of depression are biological ailments).

The problem is that the thesis of post-partum depression as a biological ailment is not compelling. In fact, the onset of this depression is usually associated with the radical hormonal changes a woman undergoes after giving birth, which does not explain how the antidepressant drugs, which claim to act — and usually claim to act selectively — on neurotransmitter levels, are considered a relevant medication. If the cause of post-partum depression is a hormonal disturbance, why should a drug thought to target neurotransmitter-based depression be prescribed?

More important, this construction of post-partum depression fails to recognize that childbirth is much more than a mere bodily event: it is the arrival of a new human life, and all the responsibility that life entails. Dr. Lynch summarizes the situation:

> While there may be a biological element to post-natal depression, this possibility has not been proven and remains purely

speculative. But the emotional upheaval associated with child-birth is not speculative; it is a fact of life. Suddenly the woman finds herself responsible for a helpless infant. Her life has changed forever. . . . Her plans for her own life have to be put on hold. While the joys of new motherhood are well recognized in society, the stresses are not. Some women find themselves with very little support. They have to cope more or less alone.[59]

Lynch expounds several other psychological factors which may be involved in a given post-partum depression, the point being that to treat the mother's emotional distress as a bodily response to a bodily event is to reduce the connected marvels of birth and motherhood to a material level.

Consequently, the personal, social and relationship changes a woman goes through during and after childbirth receive inade-quate recognition from the medical profession. . . . What women with post-natal depression need is a social, emotional and psy-chological support. Post-natal depression is not a "mental ill-ness." It is an understandable human response to one of the most challenging human experiences of all — becoming a mother.[60]

In other cases of depression, numerous accounts have been given concerning various instances of such biological reductionism. Peter Breg-gin, for example, tells of a Mrs. Pulsky who was diagnosed as a case of en-dogenous (physiologically based) depression. She was given shock therapy, which did nothing to improve her condition. With the threat of a state in-stitution looming, her family was summoned to see if their presence could achieve anything. What emerged was that Mrs. Pulsky had been repeatedly subjected to sexual abuse at the hands of her husband. Once a separation had been arranged, she was able to return home.[61]

Note how the antithetical understandings of the phenomenon of depression yield different methods of treatment. When the patient had been diagnosed with a physiological problem, she was offered electrical convul-sions as a solution, but when the doctor sought ought a more personal root of the difficulty, the true basis revealed itself. In the case of Mrs. Pulsky, if the medical team had pursued a method of simple, physiological treatment, her problematic state would never have improved. Certainly, given drugs and electroshock she might have shown fewer symptoms of her depressive state, but the internal damage done her by the abuse would have remained untended.[62]

Other individuals on antidepressants report that their new emotions appear to them strange and inappropriate to their own situation. One patient, for example "felt 'braver,' without having 'accomplished any of the lesser hurdles.' He felt Prozac was causing him to 'get ahead of himself,' and he now wondered which was the 'real' self — the one with or without Prozac."[63] Indeed, those taking antidepressants may often experience a destabilization of their own identity. "If they were themselves while taking the drug, then who were they before they took it?"[64] There is a split between the "me" who does not take antidepressants and the "me" who does.

From whence comes this sense of a separation of identities? In a normal healing process, there is no such division: I was ill, and I got better. Here it seems the movement is from "I was ill" to "I became someone else who was better." Yet this is not a proper effect of medicine. "Medication does not transform, it heals."[65] The point is that the antidepressant effects are not the result of curing physiological problems, and thus allowing the patients to respond appropriately to their lives, but are rather the outcome of neuronal stimulation brought about by the drugs. As will be shown later on, this can lead to a sharp separation within the person between an individual's cognitive apprehension of evil and the contented feelings produced by chemical manipulation. The patient's emotional and cognitive states are no longer in harmony.

It is also important to point out that not all clinicians make the error of assuming that a patient's difficulties stem solely from chemical imbalances. Certain psychiatrists do realize the role that the patient's history plays in depression. Take, for instance, Peter Kramer, who in the first chapter of his book, *Listening to Prozac*, tells of a female patient whose difficulties with depression appeared to follow naturally from her brutal past. Lacking a sufficient parental presence, the girl had basically assumed the responsibility for raising her nine younger siblings, and at a young age had married an abusive alcoholic. When her marriage fell apart, she "stumbled from one prolonged affair with an abusive married man to another."[66]

The patient thus displayed all the signs of an individual reeling from her many painful experiences. It was not, then, with an eye to curing her biological disorder that she was prescribed Prozac; the intention was rather to "terminate her depression more thoroughly, to return her to her 'premorbid self.'" Kramer adds, "Had I been working with Tess [the patient] in psychotherapy, we might have begun to explore hypotheses regarding the source of her social failure. . . . Instead, I was relegated to the surface, to what psychiatrists call the phenomena . . . . [F]or the moment, my function was to treat my patient's depression with medication."[67]

Dr. Kramer was well aware of the overwhelming evidence that the patient's problems were not caused by physiological ailments. All of his instincts told him that the patient had severe personal issues brought about by her environment. Nonetheless, his treatment was of a chemical nature, designed to affect neurotransmitters in her brain. Thus even though some clinicians may not be swayed by the biological reductionism of the popular understanding of depression, they can still be willing to prescribe the drugs in order to bring about effectively what they consider improvements.

Given the fact that to all appearances, Tess's problems seemed to spring from her personal life, what was her reaction to the drug? Although Kramer reports that his initial intention "was not to transform Tess but to restore her," he found that the drug actually altered her personality. Tess experienced "a quick alteration in ordinarily intractable problems of personality." This radical personality shift was expressed also in the change of her "circle of friends, her demeanor at work, her relationship to her family." Like the patient mentioned above, Tess also experienced a bewilderment regarding her own identity:

> Tess, too, found her transformation, marvelous though it was, somewhat unsettling. What was she to make of herself? . . . After a prolonged struggle to understand the self, to find the Gordian knot dissolved by medication is a mixed pleasure: we want some internal responsibility for our lives, want to find meaning in our errors. Tess was happy, but she talked of a mild, persistent sense of wonder and dislocation.[68]

Thus "while on Prozac, she underwent a redefinition of self."[69] After some time, an attempt was made to take Tess off the drug. After eight months she requested that she be put back on the medication. Without Prozac, she said, "I'm not myself." Clearly, her use of the medication was more than a temporary crutch to help her get back on her own feet. Now Tess associated her new identity with the effects of the pill. She was put back on Prozac, and responded again "with renewed confidence, self-assurance, and social comfort."[70]

Naturally, Dr. Kramer was concerned about the consequences of such chemical personality modification, or, in his words, "cosmetic pharmacology." "I was torn simultaneously by a sense that the medication was too far-reaching in its effects and a sense that my discomfort was arbitrary and aesthetic rather than doctorly."[71]

This is really the object of our inquiry; to determine whether Kramer's action was morally justifiable or not, and by extension, whether all doctors who prescribe antidepressants to patients whose suffering is not evidently linked to biochemistry are acting appropriately or not. What should be the principles governing morally acceptable antidepressant prescriptions, granting that no physiological basis of depression has emerged?

If a doctor can grant some form of relief with a pill, ought he hold back? He may not be fixing a biological problem, but he can still alleviate suffering and improve the patient's emotional state through chemical means. On what basis should a psychiatrist refuse antidepressants to those who want them, especially if there is no immediately apparent harm? This is the question on which we hope to shed some light in the following chapters.

Summary

Despite the widespread opinion that depression is caused by or reducible to a biochemical imbalance, the fact remains that there is no definitive evidence in support of this theory. Not only is there no currently agreed upon marker for depression, but neurophysicists have been unable to determine the mechanism by which the various drugs operate on the individual. Certainly to some degree the drugs are effective, but there is little indication that they are treating a physical malady (especially in the cases of ECT and lithium). Nonetheless, the drugs continue to be prescribed at an enormous volume, at times even for patients with evident socio-personal baggage.

    To determine whether this sort of chemical intervention on the emotional life of the patient is morally permissible, it is necessary to understand the true cause and significance of depression. The physiological explanation is unsubstantiated, so we must look elsewhere. In the next section, we will investigate the general meaning of the emotions, and of depression specifically.

II

THE ROLE OF THE EMOTIONS

But not only creativeness and enjoyment are meaningful. If there is a meaning in life at all, then there must be a meaning in suffering.

— Viktor E. Frankl, *Man's Search for Meaning*

Now that we have examined the current state of science regarding the biological aspect of depression and antidepressant drugs, it is necessary to analyze the nature of depression as a personal reality. Naturally, our understanding of depression will affect our evaluation of different forms of its treatment. Relative to modern clinical psychiatry, the normative model of depression is found in the *Diagnostic and Statistical Manual of Mental Disorders*, presently in its fourth revision (DSM IV). The manual provides the criteria for identifying depression, and is the recognized authority on the nature of that disorder for the psychiatric community as a whole. How then, does it describe depression? The answer is that all the various categories and subtypes of depression are set forth based on a symptomatic classification. So, for example, the criteria for a major depressive episode, the basic core of depression, are as follows:

A.   Five (or more) of the following symptoms have been present during the same 2-week period and represent a change from previous functioning; at least one of the symptoms is either (1) depressed mood or (2) loss of interest or pleasure.

Note: Do not include symptoms that are clearly due to a general medical condition, or mood-incongruent delusions or hallucinations.

   1).   depressed mood most of the day, nearly every day, as indicated by either subjective report (e.g., feels sad or empty) or observation made by others (e.g., appears tearful). **Note:** In children and adolescents, can be irritable mood.

2).　markedly diminished interest or pleasure in all, or almost all, activities most of the day, nearly every day (as indicated by either subjective account or observation made by others)

3).　significant weight loss when not dieting or weight gain (e.g., a change of more than 5% of body weight in a month), or decrease or increase in appetite nearly every day. **Note:** In children, consider failure to make expected weight gains.

4).　insomnia or hypersomnia nearly every day

5).　psychomotor agitation or retardation nearly every day (observable by others, not merely subjective feelings of restlessness or being slowed down)

6).　fatigue or loss of energy nearly every day

7).　feelings of worthlessness or excessive or inappropriate guilt (which may be delusional) nearly every day (not merely self-reproach or guilt about being sick)

8).　diminished ability to think or concentrate, or indecisiveness, nearly every day (either by subjective account or as observed by others)

9).　recurrent thoughts of death (not just fear of dying), recurrent suicidal ideation without a specific plan, or a suicide attempt or a specific plan for committing suicide

B.　The symptoms do not meet criteria for a Mixed Episode.

C.　The symptoms cause clinically significant distress or impairment in social, occupational, or other important areas of functioning.

D.　The symptoms are not due to the direct physiological effects of a substance (e.g., a drug of abuse, a medication) or a general medical condition (e.g., hypothyroidism).

E.　The symptoms are not better accounted for by Bereavement, i.e., after the loss of a loved one, the symptoms persist for longer than 2 months or are characterized by marked functional impairment, morbid preoccupation with worthlessness, suicidal ideation, psychotic symptoms, or psychomotor retardation.[72]

This list of the various symptoms of depression is undoubtedly of great use in clinical taxonomy; still, it must be admitted that as an actual explanation of the *nature* of depression it is far from complete. For one thing, the guidelines have, to some degree, a transparent arbitrariness. Is there no such thing as depression before a two-week period has elapsed? Why are five symptoms necessary, and not six or four? Is it so clear that grief over the passing of a loved one is disordered if it retains its intensity for nine weeks, but not for eight? The point is not to find fault with the criteria of the DSM IV; it is probably practically necessary to sort the many symptoms into different categories. To accomplish this categorization, artificial lines must sometimes be drawn. But it is important to recognize that this demarcation is based on pragmatic grounds, not on a precise analysis of the nature of depression.

This fact becomes even more evident after an examination of the second limitation of the DSM-IV's treatment of depression, namely, that it restricts itself almost entirely to a superficial exploration of the disorder. It fails to address the underlying causes and complexities of the depressed state.

> The official diagnosis of major depression leaves many questions unanswered. Most important, it does not deal with why people get depressed. . . . Is the person who is depressed [because of] irrational guilt from childhood in the same category as the person who is depressed after being caught and imprisoned for a remorseless crime?[73]

To put it otherwise, this description of depression is a phenomenological account, dealing only with its *matter*, (that is to say, with its externally apparent features) and not with its cause, essence, or finality (classically, of course, all four had to be considered before one could claim to have really understood something). In terms of the originating causes of depression, the DSM-IV, as we have noted, does not detail any specific theories, (although, regarding a biochemical hypothesis, it does concede that "No laboratory findings that are diagnostic of a Major Depressive Episode have been identified."[74])

We must, therefore, attempt to supplement this partial understanding of depression with one somewhat more holistic in its approach. For this supplement, we shall turn to the psychology of Thomas Aquinas, whose model of depression is much fuller and more intelligible and allows for a more comprehensive discussion of the proper use of antidepressant drugs. Situating depression within the category of sorrow, which is itself situated within the responsive power of the passions and the appetitive power,

Aquinas contextualizes depression within the overall taxonomy of the person as a whole. In so doing, he lays out the proper anthropological conception of the essence, causes, symptoms, and finality of depression, as well as the foundation for its appropriate treatment.

We will begin with Aquinas's understanding of the passions as a whole, since without this groundwork his treatment of depression cannot really be grasped. For our purposes, it is expedient to examine the passions as objective, as teleological, as related to physiology, and with regard to the legitimate control that the agent has over them.

The Objectivity of the Passions

For Thomas, the passions are always responses to a certain perception of reality. To cite Floyd, "Passions of the soul occur when the agent apprehends something as being attractive, unattractive, beneficial, harmful, and so forth."[75] Every passion is a reaction to something. More specifically, every passion is a reaction to some aspect of good or evil as perceived by the subject.

In fact, Aquinas distinguishes every passion, one from the other, on the basis of the different aspects of the apprehended good or evil to which the passions are a response. As might be supposed, there are many different aspects under which a thing may be perceived as good or evil. Thomas begins by saying that if a thing is perceived by the subject to be good, then the subject will experience a tendency towards that good, an affection for it. This basic tendency towards a good thing is called Love. On the other hand, if a thing is perceived by the subject to be evil, (unsuitable, unattractive), then the subject reacts with Hate for that thing, a basic inclination away from the evil. At this level the subject has yet to act; thus hate and love describe merely the existential attitude of the subject towards or away from the perceived good or evil.[76]

Should the agent move towards the perceived good, or away from the perceived evil, then the correlating passions to such states would be Desire or Aversion, respectively. Finally, when the agent acquires this sought good, the passion experienced is one of Pleasure, or Joy. By the same measure, if the subject is unable to escape from the perceived evil, he experiences Sorrow.[77]

The passions just described constitute what Aquinas calls the concupiscible passions. These are reactions to simple goods or evils, whose achievement or avoidance is accomplished without complication. Another category of passions described by Thomas, the irascible passions, are those responses to the good or evil apprehended as arduous, that is, [whose] "acquisition or avoidance involves some kind of difficulty or struggle."[78] Thus, if a good is seen to be difficult and yet possible to attain, the subject will respond to that good with Hope. If, on the other hand, the good is seen as difficult but not possible to obtain, the subject experiences Despair. Concerning reactions to evils that are difficult to avoid, one experiences Fear, and if one attempts to overcome such an evil, the passion experienced is Daring.[79]Finally, the passion Anger is a response to an evil which is already present, but against which the subject rebels.[80]

Aquinas calls these various aspects of perceived goods and evils that stimulate the passions, objects. The object of desire, then, is a good as pursued; the object of sorrow is an evil as it is present to the subject, and so forth. Thus, every passion is differentiated by its object, by which it is determined. What makes love to be love is that it has a specific object (namely, the simple perceived good), which no other passion can claim. Consequently, for Thomas the passions refer to something beyond themselves, to specific perceived realities that give the passions intelligibility. They are not simply forms of irrational energy, but on the contrary posses a distinct comprehensibility and can be categorized by the objects to which they respond. "He takes the passions to be essentially different from one another, so that they are related causally. . . ."[81] This causal relation is based on the objects to which the passions refer.

Note that when describing the objects of the passion, we refer to the goods or evils as perceived, as apprehended, as seen, and so forth. The reason for this reference is that everything eliciting aversion or attraction must be first presented under some aspect by the subject's apprehensive powers. "Appetitive reactions follow from intellectual or sensory cognitions."[82] The passions are reactions to representations of reality; in order for the subject to respond with passion to some reality, the subject will first have to detect that reality and evaluate it. So, for instance, to a hungry, healthy man, cake will be perceived as good, and thus he will respond to the cake with love and desire, and will eat it with joy. A conscientious diabetic, however, will perceive cake as severely hazardous to his health, and will instead respond to it with aversion. Thus, for one man the cake is a good object to be pursued, and for the other the cake is a bad object to be avoided. The same reality can, therefore, be either a good or bad object depending on the light in which it is seen. To quote from Claudia Eisen Murphy, "they [passions] are responses to cognitive states. They are attitudes for or against objects that have been perceived and construed as good or bad by cognition."[83]

Now this insight into the nature of the passions is extremely important in understanding the psychology of the emotions. For if the passions are indeed responses to objects that are in turn constituted by our perception of reality, then the implication is that our emotions are dependent and to some degree determined by the way in which we conceive the various elements in our experience. We can infer, then, that should the subject's evaluation of the reality in question be mistaken or crucially incomplete, the emotion produced will be likewise flawed.

Experience consistently confirms this very fact. Harak uses as the motif of his book on the passions the story of just such a mistaken evaluation, which in turn led to an inappropriate emotional reaction. He tells how a group of young men had visited a center for young boys who were either orphaned or from abusive homes. The young men, the leader of whom was named Fabian, were charitably volunteering their time in order to provide the younger boys with a sense of fraternity and positive male interaction. During a friendly soccer game, one of the boys scored a goal, and Fabian ran over to congratulate him with a pat on the back, but when the boy saw Fabian coming towards him with a raised hand, he recoiled with fear. Apparently, this child's past had led him to interpret a raised hand as a precursor to violence. He had consequently misjudged Fabian's gesture, and instead of responding with a gratitude and pleasure proper to the situation, he had instead become frightened and defensive.[84]

Naturally, this human potential to respond inappropriately, based on the erroneous evaluation of some object, has critical implications for understanding both the source and treatment of depression. For if a case of depression is caused by a misperception on the part of the subject, then surely drugs would not be the proper solution; only getting to the root of problem, namely, the erroneous judgment, could effect true healing. This application will be more thoroughly explored in a later section.

Before moving on to discuss the physicality of the emotions, it is important to note that when Aquinas speaks of the passions as being caused by judgments regarding specific objects, these judgments are not necessarily explicit evaluations, but can also be sense images and the imagination.[85] Thus, the mere sight of a beautiful woman can instinctively trigger desire in a young man, even before he has had time to formulate his desires in a conceptual judgment.[86] The same is true in the case of the imagination; passion can be *automatically* and spontaneously aroused before the subject consciously has time to evaluate the object in question. Nonetheless, the essential fact remains that the passion has responded to a certain perception/presentation of a reality as loveable or odious.

The Physicality of the Passions

For Aquinas, as we have already stated, the passions do not belong primarily to the cognitive domain, but are rather responses to some form of apprehension. Within what dimension of the person, then, ought the passions to be placed? In Thomas's system, the passions belong to the appetitive power, namely, that set of faculties concerned with attaining certain goods for the fulfillment of the agent.[87] In human beings, Thomas distinguishes two subsets of this domain, namely, the rational appetite (will) and the sensitive appetite. The rational, or intellectual, appetite is the power of attraction or repulsion from those objects apprehended by the intellect, whereas the sensitive appetite is attracted or repelled by what is perceived by the senses.[88]

Of the rational appetite and the sensitive appetite, Aquinas places the passions in the latter. According to his definition, passions, in the strict sense of the term, are to be found only where there is physical alteration.[89] One remarkable consequence of this definition is the assertion by Thomas that the passions are common to man and to irrational animals.[90] Clearly, given such a physical understanding, the passions would be more properly placed in the sensitive appetite than the spiritual.

However, Aquinas is well aware that we often refer to things like Joy, Sorrow, and Desire in cases where the object is not directly perceptible by the senses. The Joy experienced upon the receipt of a letter from a loved one is not explicable by the sensory detection of the letter's look or feel. Rather, the joy in this case is rational, intellectual joy in the symbol of the letter and the meaning of the words. A phenomenon of this kind is assuredly not common to man and the lower beasts. Further, these same attributes of joy are predicated also of God and the angels, purely spiritual realities, and hence utterly lacking senses, sense appetites, and any processes of physical change. Is it not, then, overly narrow to confine the passions to the sense appetite?

Thomas answers this exact objection in the article, "Whether Passion Is in the Sensitive Appetite Rather Than in the Intellectual Appetite, Which Is Called the Will?":

> When love and joy and the like are ascribed to God or the angels, or to man in respect of his intellectual appetite, they signify simple acts of the will having like effects, but without passion. Hence Augustine says (De Civ. Dei ix, 5): "The holy angels feel no anger while they punish . . . no fellow-feeling with misery while they relieve the unhappy: and yet ordinary human speech is wont to ascribe to them also these passions by name, because, although they have none of our weakness, their acts bear a certain resemblance to ours."[91]

Thomas is set on using the term passion in the strict sense only for those appetitive movements which involve a physical change. However, he is willing to acknowledge analogously those forms of intellectual Joy, Desire, and so forth. These rational phenomena "show a likeness to a central characteristic of sensitive emotion, namely, the approach to and withdrawal from the *conveniens* and *inconveniens* respectively."[92] Nonetheless, there can be a fundamental distinction between the passions of rational beings and those of lower animals.[93] The difference between the rational and sensitive passions is primarily the way in which the object is apprehended. If the object is perceived to be good or evil by the intellect, then the experience will differ from a case where passions follow upon the object presented as suitable or unsuitable by the senses.[94] Further, unlike the sensitive passions, the intellectual passions need not be accompanied by bodily alteration (*transmutatio corporalis*).

Thomas is aware that, due to the hylomorphic unity of the human being, certain spiritual states can *overflow* into physical effects. Thus, a good or evil that is properly the object of the intellect can, nonetheless, elicit sensitive responses. Take, for example, the often-dreaded assignment of public speaking. The individual scheduled to lecture may experience a deep fear before and sometimes during the delivery of his speech. Clearly, the fear in this case is not directed to some sensed evil, but rather to the intellectually grasped evil of criticism, failure, humiliation, and so forth. Yet many who have felt fear while speaking publicly report various physical symptoms, such as shaking knees and nausea. The reason for this reaction, according to Aquinas, would be the connection between the intellectual passion and the sensitive passion.

The point here is that Thomas allows for the correlation of bodily movements to certain psychological states, even if a particular state arises from an object that is intellectually grasped. This description fits well with the fact, suggested by certain scientific studies, that in certain cases depression coexists with some biological conditions, and yet no universal correspondence has been found.

Shawn D. Floyd goes so far as to distinguish in terminology between rational passions and sensitive passions, using emotion only for the former.[95] However, since the term "emotion" is not found in Aquinas's writings, (indeed, that word has its own unique history[96]), we will continue to use passion and emotion interchangeably to designate the movements towards both sensibly and rationally construed objects.

Control over the Passions

Given that the passions are reactions to the presentation of some reality as appropriate or inappropriate, are they simply spontaneous eruptions free from all conscious control? Can the individual command or even regulate the passions? It seems as though once the perception of an object has occurred, passion arises autonomously and independently. Yet, as Robert C. Roberts points out, apparently in certain situations an individual's affective response can be either praiseworthy or blameworthy. For example, in the case of a woman delighting in the fact that her uncle has just died, since she expects a significant inheritance, most would consider the woman's response morally deficient.[97] Yet how can one attribute fault to the passions if we are not in some way responsible for them?

Aquinas takes the position that, in fact, some measure of control over the passions is available to the person. Consequently, the passions can possess a moral aspect. "Much more, therefore, may the passions, in so far as they are voluntary, be called morally good or evil. And they are said to be voluntary, either from being commanded by the will, or from not being checked by the will."[98]

We have, then, two ways in which the person can volitionally direct the passions. Let us examine the second means first, the idea of *checking* the passions. Checking involves not giving in to the passion, denying the passion the term of its desire or aversion. Roberts gives the example of the urge to engage in illicit intercourse with a beautiful woman. This desire cannot be fulfilled, but must rather be resisted, as it is inclining toward an inappropriate object (in this case, a woman to whom the man is not married). This form of control, then, consists in a denial of "behavioral expression."[99] The passion remains frustrated in its desire, and is, therefore, externally controlled by the will. "Reason therefore holds the irascible and the concupiscible powers in check lest they proceed to an external act."[100]

The second form of control involves the *command* of rationality over the passions. "The role of reason then consists in encouraging the right passion."[101] Here, the person's objective is not so much self-restraint as a promotion of the appropriate affective response to the perceived reality. But how does one go about attempting to encourage a passion? Aquinas provides an answer based on the intellect's ability to regard a thing under different aspects:

> For since the same thing considered under different conditions can be made either pleasurable or repulsive, by means of the imagination reason lays a particular thing before sensuality under the aspect of the pleasurable or the disagreeable as it appears to reason; and so sensuality is moved to joy or to sorrow.[102]

As was stated above, the same reality can be perceived as either bad or good for the agent, depending on the light in which it is seen. Now, since one can concentrate on either the pleasing or aversive qualities of a thing, the person can to some degree control which emotions are elicited. Another example offered by Roberts:

> A beautiful meal is before you, and you're hungry. The sight and smells have fired up your sensory appetite. But then you learn that this salmon contains 400 times the maximum allowable level of dioxin. This information so affects your imagination, so embeds itself in your perception, that the food ceases to appeal to your appetite, even though in one sense it smells and looks just like it did before.[103]

The desire initially felt passes based on a new evaluation of the object in question. Thus, by means of volitional focus on a thing's good points or its bad points, the passions can be led to follow the intellect's appraisal. I can, if I wish, become angry with an old and dear friend of mine simply by consciously meditating on any unpleasing remark he might have made sometime in the past. Or, on the contrary, if someone I know has insulted me for no good reason, I might restrain myself from anger by considering the difficulties present in that individual's life.

Thomas's description of the two forms of control over the passions has some striking implications. His thesis is that we are, in fact, to some degree responsible for our emotional state. "The passions are, Thomas says, subject to moral analysis so far as they fall under the command of reason."[104] Yet how much is this simple tenet ignored in popular treatments of the emotional life? A man enters a psychiatrist's office to report homosexual longings. The poor patient, instead of receiving encouragement to restrain himself from gratifying such disordered passions (i.e., by checking the passions), may well be told something to the effect that one cannot help one's feelings, and so why not give in to them? Or suppose a woman is suffering from a general prejudice against her husband's family. She may say to herself, "Well, I'll try not to show it, but there's nothing I can do about not liking them." How much better would it be if she conscientiously made an effort to focus on the good points of the in-laws against whom she has predisposed herself (i.e., by commanding the passions)?

We are, therefore, to some extent, responsible for the governance of our emotional life. This is not meant to imply it is an easy matter. As we saw above, at times certain reactions to stimuli are elicited before we are even aware that such reactions are taking place. Further, Aquinas continues to say that the passions are only morally relevant insofar as they are under the power of reason.[105] It seems only fair to admit that in certain states we are simply not able to get address on emotions, despite our best efforts.

However, this does not excuse us from doing our utmost to try and submit our emotions to rational control.

Still, the question might arise, why is it necessary for the emotions to be subjected to proper rational guidance at all? Why not give the passions free reign, as long as one is sure to maintain a sufficient self-control in order to keep from following the passions into disordered actions? The answer is that the passions, like the other human powers, are meant to contribute to the moral goodness of persons as a whole. As motivating forces towards goods and away from evils, the passions should aid in the process of fulfillment. "Aquinas insists that our desires, pleasures, and fears need to be brought under the control of reason for a morally good life to ensue. Insofar as emotions participate in reasoning, they may intensify our moral life by becoming the instruments of moral virtue."[106]

If the inclinations are all allowed to go their separate ways, without any sense of order or cohesive unity, then the purpose of the emotions has been lost. The flourishing human being is the one whose powers have all been internally integrated and disposed to pursue goods that are fitting to the person. Unlike certain other thinkers, Aquinas does not hold that emotions necessarily lessen the freedom and, consequently, the praise or blame due an action. Rather, when the emotion is spontaneously in accord with a proper good, the person, in choosing that good, acts more holistically than would have been the case had his emotions been warring with reason.[107] The man who desires moral goodness will seek, therefore, neither to eliminate his passions, nor to allow them free reign, but will rather strive to form them so that they naturally tend to the right things.

> In other words, Thomas does not promote the rational knowledge of our passions as an ideal. He rather promotes the rationalization of the human affections, in the sense of achieving an internal permeation and not an external form of control. Thomas wants man to achieve a state in which he gives the right emotional responses to the surrounding world.[108]

Our inclinations have important teleologies, and are consequently to be used for the purposes proper to them. To experience joy at the realization of a good, and sorrow at the event of an evil is appropriate. Such is the way that man has been constituted. If, however, we are to gain a sense of internal harmony, we must struggle to mold our passions and emotions in such a way as to propel us towards moral goodness and ultimate happiness. Further, by focusing on a thing's pleasing or displeasing qualities, the intellect can promote a healthy and integrated emotional life geared towards that fulfillment that is the term of the moral life.

In order to establish the relevance of Aquinas's emotional model, it may be illuminating to mention quickly how some contemporary discoveries in the field of neuroscience support the essential Thomistic insights on affectivity. Astonishing and rapid advances in the understanding of the intricate workings of the brain have marvelously clarified and confirmed in a concrete and tangible manner the more abstract presentation of the emotions just discussed.

For example, certain studies in neuroscience attest to the intentionality of emotional experience, that is to say, the emotions' reactivity to evaluative, presentational objects, by physiologically observing how external realities are registered by areas of the brain associated with cognition, and then processed through the amygdala, whose role in emotion is coming increasingly to the fore of affective neuroscience. Joseph E. LeDoux's work on fear conditioning, to take one instance, has sought to demonstrate how a sensible object (in this case a sound) can be received through parallel neural channels, one instinctual (the auditory thalamus) and one linked with conscious analysis (the auditory cortex, related cortical areas, and the hippocampus). Both of these pathways are able, in turn, to stimulate the amygdala, and so to activate an emotional response.[109] Thus, by means of brain imaging and behavioral technique, one is able to observe in this very specific study both emotion's status as a reaction to stimulus (objectivity), as well as the distinction and relation between an emotion that reacts to instinctual detection, and an emotion that reacts to conscious evaluation (the real distinction between responses to sensible and intellectual object).

Neuroscientists have also found fascinating physiological evidence for the human capacity for control over the emotions through a focus on the pleasing or displeasing aspects of a given reality:

> In an effort to assess whether cognitive reappraisal can alter amygdala function, Ochsner and colleagues presented subjects with pictures of emotional scenes and asked them either to attend to the pictures or to reappraise the situations depicted. Consistent with previous studies, subjects rated their subjective reaction to the emotional, negative scenes as less negative on the reappraisal trials relative to attended trials. Using fMRI, Ochsner and colleagues found that the presentation of negative scenes on the attended trials resulted in more activation of the amygdala relative to the reappraisal trials.[110]

It appears that the brain itself can testify to the affective changes consequent upon conscious direction of attention; "[C]ircuits release emotions underneath the cerebral cortex, but the prefrontal cortex can learn to direct them consciously and to prevent negative feelings like sadness and fear from gaining the upper hand."[111] Further, recent discoveries about brain plasticity, that is, the brain's ability to forge new neural connections even in adulthood,[112] imply that such conscious direction of attention, with its consequent emotional response, can become physically stable, which is to say that neuroscientists seem to be uncovering the biological dimension of emotional formation.[113]

Certainly a thorough synthesis of Thomistic anthropology and the developments in the modern understanding of the brain far exceeds both my qualifications and the ambitions of this book. Nonetheless, it is both interesting and reassuring to observe in passing how well Aquinas and much of the current neuroscientific research complement each other. Both discuss how our experience of the world engenders our affective response, the similarities and differences between human and animal emotions,[114] and how we are able to form and control our feelings. Neuroscientists are able to describe in increasingly greater detail the complex physiological movements and preconditions involved in human experiences of apprehension and appetition, and by so doing to develop explicitly the incarnational aspect that pervades our lives as bodily beings. St. Thomas, for his part, demonstrates how the general powers of the soul provide the key for understanding the intelligible form and telos of man as a composite of body and spirit.

Aquinas's Discussion of Pain and Sorrow

Having given a broad overview of the passions as a whole, let us examine what Aquinas has to say about the experience of sorrow, which is certainly most relevant to the discussion of depression. As we shall see, the treatment of sorrow in the *Summa* includes a brief analysis of depression, showing how it is a natural effect of sorrow. Taking Thomas's lead, we will first examine the reality of pain and sorrow in itself, next the causes of sorrow, the effects of sorrow, and finally, the remedies of sorrow.

As stated above, the passions are divided into movements towards sensible objects and rational objects. In the domain of pain, there is also this distinction, which Aquinas confirms in terminology. He therefore uses the word "sorrow" to denote that pain which is proper to the rational creature, as opposed to "that pain which is caused by an exterior apprehension."[115] Sorrow is, therefore, a certain kind of pain, or a species of pain. He also recognizes that in common parlance "pain" is normally used to refer simply to bodily suffering, and not to the genus as a whole.[116]

Recall here that every passion is distinguished one from the other based on the object to which it refers. Just as the phenomenon of pleasure, therefore, is a reaction to a perceived present good, so sorrow responds to a perceived present evil. In this way, pleasure and sorrow are opposed to each other. Thomas does make the important point that sorrow and pleasure can, in an accidental way, cause one another:

> In one way, in so far as from sorrow at the absence of something, or at the presence of its contrary, one seeks the more eagerly for something pleasant: thus a thirsty man seeks more eagerly the pleasure of a drink, as a remedy for the pain he suffers. In another way, in so far as, from a strong desire for a certain pleasure, one does not shrink from undergoing pain, so as to obtain that pleasure.[117]

So, depending on the situation and the agent's response, pleasure may lead to the experience of a future sorrow, as pain may serve to occasion pleasure. Further, to experience sorrow does not necessarily prevent a simultaneous experience of joy, as long as they are reactions to different objects.[118] Take the case of a close friend's passing: "[T]hus a man may have sorrow at the loss of a friend, but rejoice in the fact that his friend died a holy death."[119] In this case, there is a single event in which two objects, one evil and the other good, are associated, the point being that pain and pleasure are not mutually exclusive in every situation.

The cause of sorrow or pain is the experience of a perceived evil, and yet in reality evil is nothing more than the privation of good, the inappropriate absence of a good.[120] Nonetheless, when a subject experiences sorrow, what it withdraws from is conceived of as an evil, more than as the absence of a good.[121] This is because the absence of a good is mentally reified. For example, a man scheduled to be executed in a few hours will most likely experience fear. If he is asked what it is that he fears, he will probably respond that he fears death, not that he fears the end of life, even though the two are really identical. The same is the case with sorrow, and its reaction to evil, which is really the absence of good.

Therefore, sorrow enters with the deprivation of a perceived good. When the subject apprehends a good that he wants and does not have, or that he wants and has lost, he responds with sorrow.[122] That is to say, when the craving for the union with a fulfilling thing is frustrated by some hindrance, the subject is sorrowful.[123]

What, then, is the effect of sorrow on the person as a whole? Or, to put it another way, what are the symptoms of sorrow? "From the psychological point of view, St. Thomas evidences three important effects of sorrow. Two of these are placed in the order of activity that is interior or spiritually immanent to the subject, the third, however, regards the order of transitive activity, that is, external operation."[124]

The first effect of pain, which takes place on the intellectual plane, is interference with the agent's ability to learn. The reason Aquinas gives is that the soul focuses itself on whatever pain it experiences. However, the act of learning requires adequate attention and effort. "Consequently if the pain be acute, man is prevented at the time from learning anything: indeed it can be so acute, that, as long as it lasts, a man is unable to give his attention even to that which he knew already."[125] The point is that pain and sorrow can be a distraction to the intellect, and hence can disrupt ordinary mental functioning. So, for example, a student who is having family problems at home may perform poorly in academic tasks. Such a *learning disability* need not be the result of a neurotransmitter or hormonal imbalance, or of any other physiological defects currently identified with depression, but rather a distraction impeding rational activity. "The reason is that study requires an attention that pain and sorrow effectively rob insofar as their demands overwhelm us, drawing our attention away from all other considerations, and limiting our conscious direction or comportment to only those things that pain or sorrow concern."[126] Thus, through distraction, the appetitive power can influence the normal functioning of the apprehensive power.

The next effect of sorrow dealt with by Aquinas is what he calls the "burdening of the soul," or "depression."

> For a man is said to be depressed, through being hindered in his own movement by some weight. Now it is evident from what has been said above that sorrow is caused by a present evil: and this evil, from the very fact that it is repugnant to the movement of the will, depresses the soul, inasmuch as it hinders it from enjoying that which it wishes to enjoy.[127]

Aquinas explains sorrowful depression as a state of being restricted from goodness. The individual is "weighed on" by whatever present evil is imposed upon it. Such a constricted soul, "through being depressed so as to be unable to attend freely to outward things, withdraws to itself, closing itself up as it were."[128]

Here it is important to pause and consider the self-enclosing quality of depression. What does Thomas mean when he states that the depressed soul is "unable to attend freely to outward things?" His point is simply that in certain cases, the sorrow that reacts to a specific evil extends its influence to the other human faculties engaged with the world around us, namely, the faculties of apprehension and appetite. The person is so busy responding to one form of evil, that it becomes difficult or impossible to perceive effectively and react to the surrounding environment. Suppose a severe tragedy has recently befallen me, let us say the unexpected death of my young daughter. Suppose further that a few days after this terrible event, a colleague at work, unaware of my cause for grief, rushes into my office and excitedly informs me that I have just received a much hoped-for promotion. Although a short time before this news would have given me great delight, my present sorrow is such that I barely comprehend the message of my co-worker, and react to it with complete indifference.

This is the state of depression articulated by Aquinas: due to an intense focus on sorrow, interaction with other facets of life becomes inhibited, to greater or lesser degrees, such that the soul becomes internally oriented. This sort of attitude is evident in people who report "feeling blue," who simply cannot take significant interest in anything, and who no longer possess a lust for life. Thomas understands such a condition to be symptomatic of an underlying sorrow over a good of which the subject is deprived.

In fact, Thomas goes so far as to assert that sorrow or pain can affect all forms of activity, "for we never do that which we do with sorrow, so well as that which we do with pleasure, or without sorrow." Aquinas's account of the symptoms proper to depression consequently correspond closely to many of the signs used currently to identify the "disorder," that is, "depressed mood, (such as feelings of sadness)," "reduced interest in activities," "loss of energy or a significant reduction in energy level," and "difficulty concentrating."[129]

Yet his insight into the debilitating effects of depression is balanced with the assertion that certain actions actually are encouraged by sorrow, insofar as there is a hope to be rid of such suffering.[130] As long as one can resist despair, sorrow can serve as an impetus to better one's situation. If, however, the evil appears so strong as to exclude any hope of escape, "then even the interior movement of the afflicted soul is absolutely hindered, so that it cannot turn aside either this way or that."[131] For Aquinas, the phenomenon of despair is a perpetual state of depression, with no end in sight.

After such an analysis of the traumatic and sometimes devastating effects of sorrow, the student of Aquinas might be surprised to find that he does not consider sorrow itself a bad thing. True, sorrow presumes some form of privation, some evil, some hindrance of good. There cannot be sorrow unless something undesirable has occurred, as has already been shown. Nonetheless, the phenomenon of sorrow itself cannot be identified with the evil that causes it. Sorrow is an apprehension of and an aversion to a present evil, and as such it is an appropriate human response. In fact, Aquinas states that the failure to react with sorrow or pain to a perceived evil implies some deficit in the agent. "For if he were not to be in sorrow or pain, this could only be either because he feels it not, or because he does not reckon it as something unbecoming, both of which are manifest evils. Consequently it is a condition of goodness, that, supposing an evil to be present, sorrow or pain should ensue."[132]

Aquinas goes on to explain that appropriate sorrow is, in fact, a form of virtue, or a "rectitude of reason and will."[133] For both the apprehensive and appetitive facets of the person are brought into play with sorrow, just as with every other passion/emotion. If the individual accurately perceives an evil reality, then such an act of awareness is virtuous, as it involves a perfection of a certain power, in this case the power of discernment. By the same token, if the individual responds to the evil with repugnance, such distaste indicates a well-formed appetite.

This is not to say that all sorrow is necessarily virtuous. Sometimes the operations of intellect and will are critically flawed, such that something good is perceived as evil, or reacted to as though it was undesirable. To take an example of the first, in a culture where cows are considered sacred creatures, the eating of beef would be perceived as an evil, and would hence be accompanied by sorrow. Or, to take an image from Aquinas, the man who gives alms sorrowfully is not experiencing virtuous sorrow. Presumably such a man knows that almsgiving is an appropriate good, and yet he reacts to it as though it were evil. This shows at least some level of imperfection in the tither's will. Lastly, Thomas's Aristotelian understanding of virtue (or at least, of non-theological virtues) as a balance between extremes, allows him to recognize that there can be excessive sorrow, sorrow that is disproportionate to the gravity of the offending evil. An extreme reaction of this kind also "fails to be a virtuous good."[134]

However, Aquinas states that even though sorrow be defective in some way, it is not the ultimate misfortune. For if the individual is sorrowful over something that is in fact a good, and not an evil, then at least the real state of the person involves a union with the good thing in question. And to be united with goodness, in whatever manner, is fulfilling to man, is proper to him, and is a perfection of his nature.[135]

Nor should one conclude from Aquinas's defense of sorrow that he encourages a state of dejected resignation. Indeed, Thomas would have little patience with a self-indulgent gloominess. Sorrow is most certainly not to be sought for sorrow's sake. On the contrary, a virtuous sorrow is always constructive, always linked to an impetus toward improvement. In this latter sense does Aquinas commend sorrow as a useful good:

> A twofold movement of the appetite ensues from a present evil.
> One is that whereby the appetite is opposed to the present evil;

and, in this respect, sorrow is of no use; because that which is present cannot be not present. The other movement arises in the appetite to the effect of avoiding or expelling the saddening evil: and, in this respect, sorrow is of use, if it be for something which ought to be avoided.[136]

A sorrow that does no more than bemoan a present state of affairs, is, according to Aquinas, "of no use."[137] Rather, sorrow is meant to propel the individual to evade or oust the undesirable situation or element in question. This movement, this urge to better one's state of affairs, is the telos of sorrow. For sorrow is brought about by some evil, and one who suffers should be roused by his emotional state to distance himself from evil (or, as Thomas notes, sometimes even from that which would serve as an occasion for evil). So sorrow actually serves as a motivating force toward action, or, to put the matter more paradoxically, suffering is intended to give man purpose. If a man is able, by his effort, to relieve himself of pain, whether spiritual or physical, his effort will be all the more in earnest due to suffering.[138]

Thomistic Therapies in Relation to Sorrow

From this basic outline of Aquinas's treatment of sorrow in itself and in its effects, let us turn to what might be considered his *therapeutic* section. As we have seen, passions and emotions can at times assume undesirable excesses, and sorrow is no exception. It was also shown, however, that it is reason's task to moderate these inordinate movements. Given Thomas's characteristic thoroughness, then, it is hardly surprising that he should include some practical advice about how this is best accomplished. What is remarkable is the holism of the suggested techniques for diminishing sorrow. For a solitary friar born some six hundred years prior to the advent of modern psychology, his method of targeting the various relevant dimensions of a human being in order to abate extreme sorrow or pain is most striking. Indeed, he includes in his prescribed measures what today might be termed "cognitive," "affective," and "ventilation" therapies.

Beginning on the general scale, Thomas starts out with the premise that pleasure of any kind can serve to alleviate sorrow to some degree. Sorrow is a reaction of the appetite to some defect of goodness, while pleasure is a reaction of the appetite to some fullness of good. Therefore, where there is real pleasure there is at least some satiation of the person's desire for goodness, and so the cause of sorrow, (that is, a lack of satiation, an estrangement from good), is lessened.[139] "Pleasure, however, is a sort of quiet of the same inclination in the possession of the good, and therefore it is, in a certain way, a restorative to that unnatural fatigue [of the frustrated appetite]."[140] With the experience of pleasure, the person is somehow made less empty, and, therefore, less sorrowful.

Concerning the specific pleasures articulated by Aquinas that are of help to the suffering, the first mentioned, the act of weeping, is not commonly associated with pleasure. Nonetheless, Thomas is clear in stating that weeping in times of sorrow is itself a soothing pleasure, for two reasons:

> First, because a hurtful thing hurts yet more if we keep it shut up, because the soul is more intent on it: whereas if it be allowed to escape, the soul's intention is dispersed as it were on outward things, so that the inward sorrow is lessened. This is why men, burdened with sorrow, make outward show of their sorrow, by tears or groans or even by words, their sorrow is assuaged. Secondly, because an action, that befits a man according to his actual disposition, is always pleasant to him. Now tears and groans are actions befitting a man who is in sorrow or pain; and consequently they become pleasant to him. Since then, as stated above, every pleasure assuages sorrow or pain somewhat, it follows that sorrow is assuaged by weeping and groans.[141]

The first reason as to why tears are therapeutic involves the fact that external expression can help a man escape from the dangers of depression, in which state the individual retreats into himself and loses contact with the surrounding world. Thomas seems to say that tears are a manifestation of grief in a bodily manner, thus reconnecting the person's interior and exterior life. The very act of weeping by its nature guards against the sufferer becoming enclosed within himself, since the shedding of tears transcends the purely intentional dimension of the subject. Thus, one who weeps allows his experience to open up and go outside of himself, preventing the degenerate state of sorrowful narcissism.

Aquinas's second argument is based on the fact that "tears and groans are actions befitting a man who is in sorrow or pain; and consequently, they become pleasant to him." Thomas's basic premise, therefore, is that whatever is proper to a person is pleasing to him: "[E]very effect is suited to its cause, and consequently is pleasant to it."[142] Thus, when a cause achieves its natural effect, pleasure results, whereas this pleasure would be lacking if the cause were to be frustrated in the production of its effect. Sorrow naturally produces tears, and consequently, when tears in fact are elicited, the person is pleased on that account, which in turn lessens his overall sorrow.

Another suggested aid for the diminishment of sorrow is the sympathy of friends. Here, as in the case of weeping, there are two advantages to the sufferer who receives sympathy. The first is that in the experience of sympathy, those sympathizing seem to help the sufferer by sharing in his grief. Aquinas is here content to return to the image of sorrow as a load, which is more easily borne by many than by just one. This sort of remedy targets the passion itself, by seeking to alleviate that passion through compassion. Further, sympathy is helpful in that it provides the sufferer with the knowledge that he is loved and, possesses true friends. This realization is a source of great pleasure to him, which in turn decreases sorrow.

Thomas also recognizes the benefits of bodily goods in terms of mitigating pain and sorrow.[143] Granted, sorrow is an affliction of the soul, whereas such things as sleep and baths (the two physical goods he mentions) give pleasure to the body. This raises the question, how can physical pleasure lend aid to spiritual pain? The response lies in the human person's composite nature, uniting and integrating body and soul. As we saw in dealing with the distinction and interaction of the passions and the emotions, bodily states can influence the soul, and vice versa. Hence the pleasure that accompanies the fulfillment of some physical dimension can grant relief to psychological suffering. "The normal disposition of the body, so far as it is felt, is itself a cause of pleasure, and consequently assuages sorrow."[144]

In looking at Aquinas's treatment on the physical alleviations of sorrow, Stephen Loughlin considers how Aquinas would have reacted to antidepressant drugs, which are said to "address the specific bodily changes in sorrow." Loughlin concludes that although Aquinas would be open to certain positive aspects of these medications, since the cause of sorrow is an evaluative judgment, a drug would not in itself provide an ultimate solution to sorrow. "[T]he fact still remains that Thomas would consider a drug targeting the very center of the body's involvement in sorrow as a particularly strong mitigating factor of sorrow's effects, but still as something which addresses only the symptoms, and not sorrow's underlying causes. The remedy for sorrow, in Aquinas's view, is not a material one."[145] Physiological measures may be of great service, but alone they will prove insufficient.

Here it is of use to pause and reflect on these last three aids against sorrow articulated by Aquinas. Clearly, it would be a grave mistake to identify Thomas as a cold, distant, speculative therapist, interested only in the truth/error content of his patients' psychological state. The techniques of emotional expression, sympathy, and bodily pleasures all contribute to the healing of the one burdened with excessive sorrow. In fact, given Thomas's support of baths and sleep, it is not unreasonable to suppose that he would have recognized the benefits of practices like aroma therapy and massage.

The point is that Thomas's advised treatments for spiritual suffering are not in any way limited to the propositional level, but include a much more multifaceted approach.

This recognition does not imply that Thomas neglects to discuss a therapy on the intellectual level. After all, he has offered a remedy of sorrow through its effect (tears), and remedies that target sorrow directly (sympathy and pleasure in general). It should, consequently, come as no surprise that he should propose a remedy of sorrow through its cause, namely, the cognitive state from whence the sorrow arises. As we have seen, for Thomas the emotions in general and sorrow in particular are responses to an intellectual apprehension of reality. Consequently, therapy could not be integrated if it failed to address the sufferer's perception of his own environment.

It is interesting to observe that the first benefit of the contemplation of truth Aquinas discusses continues his theme of pleasure. Since for Aquinas, the contemplation of truth is the fulfillment or actualization of the power of the intellect, it is a great good, in fact the greatest, and thus affords man a very great pleasure,[146] which in turn works toward a diminishment of sorrow.[147] Therefore, just the *act* of knowing is pleasant to the knower, even if what is known is in itself not pleasing.[148] Here the advantage derives simply from the act of knowledge, and not necessarily from the content of that knowledge.

Yet Thomas also complements this understanding with a powerful affirmation of the pleasing aspects of the *content* of knowledge. He states:

> And therefore in the midst of tribulations men rejoice in the contemplation of Divine things and of future Happiness, according to James 1:2: "My brethren, count it all joy, when you shall fall into divers temptations": and, what is more, even in the midst of bodily tortures this joy is found; as the martyr Tiburtius, when he was walking barefoot on the burning coals, said: "Methinks, I walk on roses, in the name of Jesus Christ."[149]

Here we have a diminishment of sorrow, in fact a remedy by which all sorrows can be borne, which issues from the content of knowledge itself, from the truth and reality that is contemplated. If every emotional state comes from some perception of reality, then this joy that is a sure counter to distress comes from the Christian vision of the world, or in Aquinas's words, "the contemplation of Divine things and of future Happiness." This contemplation not only soothes psychological suffering, but can even serve as a balm for the afflictions of the body, such is the pleasure produced by thinking about the truths of the Faith.

If this is so, if the Christian vision of the universe is ultimately pleasing, it can only be because it presents a world that is fundamentally good, fundamentally worthwhile, meaningful, hopeful, and fulfilling. Thomas could only offer the doctrines of Christianity as uniquely useful in the fight against sorrow if they provided a presentation of goodness, of the decisive victory of goodness over evil. To put it another way, a proper and realistic understanding of the human condition (an understanding possible only through faith), leads to a healthy and well-grounded joy, even in the face of present evils. Conversely, extreme sorrow or even despair is the result of an erroneous and overly pessimistic view of the world. Contemplation of the true state of affairs, (always maintaining a proper perspective), consequently effects a balanced formation of the emotional life.

Summary

The model of the passions/emotions found in the writings of Thomas Aquinas sheds great light on the reality of depression, which is a specification of sorrow, which is in turn a movement of the appetitive power. Up until this point, we have spoken at some length about the nature of the emotions as responsive to "perception," "judgment," or "evaluation." (In Aquinas's words, "For the appetitive power is . . . naturally moved by the thing apprehended."[150]) Here it is important to guard against a dangerous misunderstanding that these perceptions, judgments, and evaluations are always reasonable, accurate, or conscious. That a patient's evaluations are not necessarily explicit or well-articulated propositions cannot be emphasized too strongly, nor are they always accurate or reasonable. This is why, as the analysis of the passions in general and sorrow in particular sought to demonstrate, the emotional life of many people is disordered and disproportionate to their situation. For a person to have an unbalanced affective response to relatively inconsequential events, such as seasonal changes, is possible.[151] *Their emotions have not been properly subjected to right reason.* They are responding to evaluation, but not to reasonable evaluation. Emotions react to evaluations, and if the evaluation is flawed so, too, will be the reaction. Consequently, it should not be surprising for many cases of depression to be based on irrational judgments.

Aquinas's therapeutic remedies, while obviously not intended to be comprehensive, nonetheless provide a foundation and framework for the treatment of excessive or disordered sorrow. The holism of his method, engaging the affective, cognitive, expressive, interpersonal, and even bodily needs of the sufferer, manifests the richness of the Thomistic understanding of the human self. Further, and what is more to the point in the present study, all of the pleasures suggested to decrease sorrow come from real, present goods, which are recognized by the subject as such. The individual perceives these positive realities, which range from baths to meditations on salvation history, and responds to them with delight, thus attempting to mitigate disproportionate sorrow. To try and reform our emotions by such means in accord with the judgments of right reason is our obligation.

Among the effects of sorrow, Aquinas lists depression, a phenomenon in which the individual retreats within himself, disassociating the self from the surrounding environment. Depression is not, therefore, an unintelligible, senseless ailment, and one need not turn as by default to the physical makeup of the person in order to understand its origin. Rather, it generally seems to stem from an excessive introspection and concentration on internal pain. This state is to be especially fought by attempting to reconnect the person with what might be called extra-mental reality (the emotional expression of weeping is especially recommended). Whatever methods are used, any effective therapy of depression must understand and respond to the suffering of which depression is an effect, and Aquinas offers a basic structure for comprehending and treating sorrow in general. To quote again from Loughlin:

> Based, then, upon the description that Aquinas offers of sorrow, and the depths to which one may sink with respect to it, it is a fair thing to say that Aquinas does indeed articulate a robust notion of depression, one which speaks directly and intelligently to the human condition, to the real experience of it, and beyond it to the frightening depths to which it can plunge a person who is not careful to prevent the overwhelming and transforming effects that sorrow brings with it.[152]

However, one possible counterargument to Aquinas's treatment of depression is the characterization of the disorder as a *mood*, an experience of feelings which has no directionality or deeper intelligibility. Perhaps depression is simply a state of general displeasure, not in itself referable to any cognitive origin or term. Is it not possible that we just sometimes feel depressed without any real reason? In other words, it is not immediately evident that for every affective condition we must posit an intentional object. Mark P. Drost makes the distinction quite explicitly: "Experiences which do not have objects, such as depression, are *moods* and are distinct from emotions. Moods do not exhibit the intentional focus that emotions exhibit."[153] Yet if this assumption were so, if certain feelings were not directly related to the reactive energy of the person to an object, it would gravely undermine the completeness of Aquinas's psychology, and of his understanding of depression in particular.

Certainly, to speak of depression as a mood, an affective experience lacking directionality towards an object, is not incoherent, just as it is not incoherent to speak of depression as a biochemical imbalance. Nonetheless, I believe that the Thomistic account of depression is at once more meaningfully integrated within the rest of human experience and more richly teleological than either conception. His exposition of the intentionality of all feelings affords a clear picture of the essence of depression as a movement of the appetitive power (formal cause) stimulated by and geared toward a perceived good or a perceived evil (efficient and final cause) with various psycho-somatic manifestations (material cause).

This is not to deny the usefulness of distinguishing moods, like depression, as subsets within the broader spectrum of emotion, which is precisely Aquinas's approach. He describes depression as a potential mode of sorrow that is distinct from other forms of sorrow in that it extends itself in reference not only to this thing or that thing, but to things in general. This extension sets a mood apart from other affective experience; its object becomes extremely generalized. Even Drost admits the feasibility of moods' uniqueness lying in the fact that "their intentional bearing is too global to characterize in terms of an intentional focus."[154] The term global is apt, for a mood like depression intends not one object or another, but rather its object is the world as a whole. "Depression is a psychological state — an emotional response to life."[155] Moods are different from other emotions, not because they lack an object, but because their object is so vast in scope.

In any event, the Thomistic perspective brings the true significance of sorrow and depression to the foreground. It is perhaps appropriate to sum up Thomas's discussion on sorrow with the following quotation: "Pain or sorrow for that which is truly evil cannot be the greatest evil: for there is something worse, namely, either not to reckon as evil that which is really evil, or not to reject it."[156] When placed in the context of a society that considers pain and sorrow meaningless, useless, and to be avoided at all costs, this statement takes on a massive relevance. Experiencing an inappropriate reality not accompanied by sorrow entails a corruption of human nature that lowers the person on the overall scale of perfection and goodness. Separation from sorrow is not in itself desirable, since a state of complacency that fails to recognize and react to evil is a mark of personal deficiency. Certainly false sorrows are to be avoided, as are undue excesses, and yet as with all the emotion, pain on both the physical and spiritual level has an important function in our earthly life, and should, therefore, be respected and guided by reason in a manner that will unify the human person and lead to his greater fulfillment.

III

Basic Moral Principles

> For God is not offended by us except by what we do against our own good.
>
> — Thomas Aquinas, *ScG*, 122

At this point, it is necessary to formulate the basic principles for how man's various capacities are to be treated if he is to achieve the fulfillment and perfection proper to his being. Without recourse to the fundamental moral guidelines for respecting and ennobling human nature, the proper steward-ship of the emotions cannot be articulated. Hence, this section will attempt to describe the maxims from which more specific precepts can be derived, notably precepts concerning proper emotional management, which will in turn shed light on the issues surrounding the use of antidepressants.

An appropriate beginning is the basic understanding of morality as the art of fulfilling the *human person*, of making the *human person* as perfect as he can possibly be, of attaining all those goods appropriate to one's nature in order to maximize one's potential for excellence.

> "[O]ur moral life, if viewed from the perspective of a person seeking to be morally upright, can be described as an endeavor, cognitively, to come to know what we are to do if we are to be fully the beings we are meant to be, and cognitively, to do what we ourselves come to know we are to do if we are to become fully the beings we are meant to be."[157]

Such a conception of the moral life is dramatically diverse both from a re-jection of the objective and binding nature of moral truth as well as from value-systems that divorce ethical norms from the movement toward human flourishing.[158] Rather, the whole goal and scope of the moral life is to know and do what we must to fulfill ourselves as perfectly as possible.

> Despite all conceptual differentiations, the variety of historical
> contexts, and the difference of accentuation among the various
> thinkers, these approaches agree on the decisive point: the issue
> in moral action is not some relationship between external goods
> or the sum of these, but whether the human being succeeds or
> fails in his human existence and his quality as a person.[159]

With the gift of faith, moreover, we become aware not only of the ultimate
source and foundation of our inherent teleology, but also of an infinitely
greater degree of perfection that the human person, with the help of divine
grace, can attain. We are further informed concerning the specifics of divine
intervention for our sake, as well as the unique tools and aids God has given
us as a help in reaching the end He has willed for us. This supernatural
goal, which includes and infinitely surpasses the fulfillment due our natural
state, can only be effectively sought with a simultaneous respect for both
the natural and supernatural capacities of the human being. For the informed and sincere Catholic, religious obligations will never demand a
contortion of the nature upon which grace builds. Rather, the believer —
like the unbeliever — is obliged by the dictates of nature to integrally pursue human flourishing, such that all his faculties harmoniously work toward
the good. This integrated character of the excellent human being has tradi-
tionally been termed "virtue," and it expresses the state in which the person
has constituted himself to act naturally and spontaneously in appropriate
and self-perfective ways.

     Our hope here is not so much to provide a system that demonstrates
how this human integrity is to be positively nurtured and strengthened;
rather, the goal is more negative in the sense of determining how integral
flourishing is to be safeguarded and protected from threat of attack. What
guidelines are to be used in preserving man from all affronts to his natural
dignity? How is it possible to recognize such affronts? Once these questions
have received some response, we will be better situated to determine
whether antidepressants carry the threat of injury to personal well-being.

The Principle of Integrity

All of man's actions are ordered towards goodness, and toward what the
individual believes will be fulfilling for him. Nonetheless, even though one
intends to bring about some personal human good, one can act in a way
that directly attacks human goodness on another level. For example, suppose two men are courting the same woman, and one of the suitors murders
the other in order to eliminate his competition. Clearly, the goal of the mur-
derer is a fulfilling good, namely, the interpersonal love proper to a man

and a woman. Yet, in fact, the suitor's chosen course of action directly attacks the good of interpersonal communion on another level, namely, the bond of charity, which should unite all persons. The suitor's natural human capacity to love his fellow man is stifled by his murderous decision, thus attacking human goodness in order to achieve human goodness. The action is, therefore, morally unacceptable.

To violate and frustrate the nature of the human being intentionally, to go against the proper purposes and functions of the person, can never be morally permitted, as it goes against authentic fulfillment and flourishing. Even if circumstances are dire, one must be cautious against the temptation of teleological ethics or consequentialism, systems that seek to determine the morality of actions based on the good or bad effects that are foreseen to occur from the individual action in question.[160] As Martin Rhonheimer has expertly shown, this system fundamentally fails due to its lack of a criterion for the ordering of consequences.[161] The result is that consequentialists are unable to recognize certain actions whose consequences "cannot be accepted, no matter what other consequences may be foreseen."[162] Such actions are those classically termed "intrinsically evil," and which, according to the constant tradition of magisterial theology, may never be morally permitted, regardless of the situation. The question that must be asked when evaluating a given action must always be, "Does it violate the person, and consequently inhibit him from the task with which God has entrusted him, namely, fulfillment of self and neighbor?" For if it does, then regardless of all other anticipated consequences, it is a sinful act by which we pervert ourselves and displease the Author of human nature.

This does not mean we are obliged to develop every potential for flourishing simultaneously or even to the same degree. One may choose in individual actions to fulfill certain capacities instead of others. For example the choice of celibate priesthood normally involves the impossibility of developing one's capacity for marital love. Yet here there is no aggression against the good of marital love, simply a decision not to pursue it. The celibate does not transgress the basic precept (which we will call the "principle of integrity") forbidding any direct willing or assault against the fundamental structure of the human person or those goods that constitute fulfillment for him.

Magisterial Pronouncements against Certain Violations of Human Integrity

Due to the psychosomatic unity of a human being, acts can be performed upon the body that do, in fact, injure the person by frustrating his progress toward perfection. Here we enter the realm of bioethics, where particular uses or manipulations of the body must be examined to see whether they are compatible with the overall well-being of the person. As we have seen, and as must be kept in mind when considering the specific issue of mood-altering medications, in a moral analysis it is not simply the physical health of the person that must be considered, but the integrity and wholeness of the soul. In our current study concerning possible misuses of antidepressant drugs, the critical question is, "How does one recognize violations against personal integrity? What are the signs that the goodness of human nature has been attacked?"

To some degree, any recognition of a moral offense will demand a fundamental insight into the proper purpose and harmonious functionality of the human being, and consequently into what behavior is detrimental to that purpose and functionality. This reliance on fundamental insight implies that ultimately no moral precept can be reached through inferential argumentation,[163] but rather by appeals to basic perception of human nature and its potential to flourish. However, one can facilitate such insight and perception by analyzing various examples of already articulated offenses against human nature, and the specific harm they cause. Thus, by *practicing* the art of recognizing attacks on personal goodness, one begins to see a trend in the different cases that can then be applied to other issues. Here, I believe, examining certain magisterial precepts against very specific actions is worthwhile, in order to illustrate how these actions are forbidden because of their direct affront against human integrity.

Due to the intense controversy surrounding the issue of contraception, the papal teaching regarding its unacceptability is extremely developed and explicit, making it conducive to our purposes. It will also be a convenient model when seeking to apply the same principles to antidepressant usage.

In *Humanae Vitae*, Paul VI begins with a candid consideration of the appealing features of contraceptive use, and even whether the principle of totality might serve to justify acts of sterilization that would contribute to the greater good of persons on the whole. Nonetheless, he states, the answer to this problem can only be discovered in light of an appreciation of holistic human teleology: "The problem of birth, like every other problem regarding human life, is to be considered, beyond partial perspectives — whether of the biological or psychological, demographic or sociological orders — in the light of an integral vision of man and of his vocation, not only his natural and earthly, but also his supernatural and eternal vocation."[164] The Pope disagrees with any who might classify human reproduction as a merely biological phenomenon; this issue must be discussed in the context of man's comprehensive reality. Otherwise — if some aspect of human nature is ignored — the risk of fragmentation is run, and personal integrity will be compromised. Although there may be a great many motivations for pursuing a given course of action, in order to determine if that act is really permissible, one must first make certain that no violence is done to the person's capacity for excellence, be it natural or supernatural. The principle of integrity must be thoughtfully applied to the action, and if the action does in fact go against that principle, it is de facto contrary to the moral order. For "it is not licit, even for the gravest reasons, to do evil so that good may follow therefrom; that is, to make into the object of a positive act of the will something which is intrinsically disordered, and hence unworthy of the human person, even when the intention is to safeguard or promote individual, family or social well-being."[165] In contrast to the doctrines of consequentialism, *Humanae Vitae* is firm in its conviction that no expected outcome, however good in itself, can justify the performance of a morally evil act, that is, an act that diminishes the basic goodness of human beings.

This leads Paul VI to a treatment of marital love as a good that is fulfilling of the whole human person. Further, he clarifies that this love affects the entire person: "This love is first of all fully human, that is to say, of the senses and of the spirit at the same time. It is not, then, a simple transport of instinct and sentiment, but also, and principally, an act of free will. . . ."[166] Since human sexuality is an elevated power, one that intimately involves the spiritual capacities as well as the physical, to frustrate or pervert it would offend against the person as a whole, and would, therefore, break the moral directive to safeguard human integrity.

It should be plain, then, that papal understanding of contraception is not based simply on observations concerning the biological structure of human sexuality. On the contrary, Paul VI's historic treatment of human sexuality is based on the insight that it uniquely expresses and determines the spiritual constitution of the human being.

Humanae Vitae expounds two basic personal goods towards which human sexuality is intrinsically oriented. The first is the union of husband and wife, "in such a way that husband and wife become one only heart and one only soul, and together attain their perfection."[167] Obviously, this union goes beyond the mere physical joining that takes place in conjugal relations, for it is an intense form of interpersonal communion, in which the souls of the partners unite in a mutually fulfilling love. In articulating the second good of marital intercourse, the pontiff quotes from Vatican II's *Gaudium et Spes*: "Marriage and conjugal love are by their nature ordained toward the begetting and educating of children. Children are really the supreme gift of marriage and contribute very substantially to the welfare of their parents."[168] The second personal good of the sexual act, therefore, is the generation and nurturing of children. This good is perfective of the husband and wife; it contributes "very substantially" to their fulfillment. Human sexuality, therefore, is a human capacity for a unique perfection involving spousal communion and the procreation of human life, both of which are, according to the magisterium, goods that enable the person to flourish.

Such is the nature of the marital act. It is its meaning, its telos. In this way, the man and woman have been made by their Creator, and consequently His will is manifested in the design of human sexuality:

> In the task of transmitting life, therefore, they [husband and wife] are not free to proceed completely at will, as if they could determine in a wholly autonomous way the honest path to follow; but they must conform their activity to the creative intention of God. . . . That teaching, often set forth by the magisterium, is founded upon the inseparable connection, willed by God and unable to be broken by man on his own initiative, between the two meanings of the conjugal act: the unitive meaning and the procreative meaning. Indeed, by its intimate structure, the conjugal act, while most closely uniting husband and wife, capacitates them for the generation of new lives, according to laws inscribed in the very being of man and of woman.[169]

Man did not create himself, but rather finds himself and the world around him to have a definite structure, with the conditions for perfection and flourishing already determined. As he is not able to change his own basic structure, so he is unable to reinvent the conditions for his own fulfillment. These decisions have been made independently of his will, and he can but accept them. Nonetheless, the choice offered to the human being is still of great significance, for he can decide whether or not to actualize those conditions, to self-perfect or to bring about his own degeneration. The former choice involves a conformation to the demands of our nature, and fundamentally, to the will of God, who is responsible for the essence of humanity being what it is.

In the case of sexuality, that which is given to man by nature, and consequently by God, is a power that is intended to lead to union and procreation. The meaning of this power is, in the words of Paul VI, "inscribed in the very being of man and of woman." To attempt to use the power while intentionally preventing the achievement of its teleological function is, in fact, to thwart and do damage to the power in question, and hence to cause degeneration to the whole person. As contraception is a direct attempt to rid one's sexuality of its procreative dimension, it is an offense against human nature and the Creator's design. "To use this divine gift destroying, even if only partially, its meaning and its purpose is to contradict the nature both of man and of woman and of their most intimate relationship, and therefore it is to contradict also the plan of God and His will."[170] Although there may be a great number of motives for the use of contraceptives, the price, namely the loss of man's functional integrity, is too great, and will ultimately detract from the overall well-being of the person. "...[M]an cannot find true happiness — toward which he aspires with all his being — other than in respect of the laws written by God in his very nature, laws which he must observe with intelligence and love."[171] In the next section, we will discuss how this exact reasoning, when applied to *certain* uses of antidepressants, logically leads to similar condemnations.

Paul VI's reasoning is echoed in the writings of the late Holy Father, John Paul II, most notably in the encyclical, *Familiaris consortio*. Here it is sufficient to provide a single citation that shows the continuity and development of the thought expressed in *Humanae Vitae*. Again, the emphasis in this excerpt is on avoiding the error of viewing sexuality from a merely physiological viewpoint:

> Consequently, sexuality, by means of which man and woman give themselves to one another through the acts which are proper and exclusive to spouses, is by no means something purely biological, but concerns the innermost being of the human person as such. It is realized in a truly human way only if it is an integral part of the love by which a man and a woman commit themselves totally to one another until death. The total physical self-giving would be a lie if it were not the sign and fruit of a total personal self-giving. . . . This totality which is required by conjugal love also corresponds to the demands of responsible fertility. This fertility is directed to the generation of a human being, and so by its nature it surpasses the purely biological order and involves a whole series of personal values.[172]

John Paul II, like his predecessor, recognizes that the act that includes both bodily union and the possibility of bodily reproduction entails also the spiritual dimension of the human being, and therefore possesses a special personal significance. Such spiritual capacities may not be directly devalued, and so the Holy Father is obliged to recognize the impermissibility of any intentional obstruction of the procreative facet of human sexuality.

We have, then, regarding contraception, a very clear line of moral reasoning in the papal encyclicals that perceives a certain human capacity for goodness and condemns any willful frustration of that capacity. The personal functions of sexual union and procreation are not to be disfigured or robbed of their proper ends; to do so involves a degradation of the human being.[173] Nor, we may anticipate, are the personal functions of the emotions, specifically sorrow, to be disfigured or robbed of their proper ends, as a similar degradation would result.

As shown, the magisterial theology of human integrity and its preservation comes into especially sharp focus in pronouncements against contraception, and yet other forms of offenses against the person have also been singled out for condemnation. A concise and yet very substantial list of such offenses can be found in the documents of the Second Vatican Council:

> All offenses against life itself, such as murder, genocide, abortion, euthanasia and willful self-destruction; all violations of the integrity of the human person, such as mutilation, physical and mental torture, undue psychological pressures; all offenses against human dignity, such as subhuman living conditions, arbitrary imprisonment, deportation, slavery, prostitution, the selling of women and children, degrading work conditions where men are treated as mere tools for profit rather than free and responsible persons; all these and their like are criminal; they poison civilization; and they debase their perpetrators more than their victims and militate against the honor of the Creator.[174]

In this list we see a variety of actions, be they sexual, violent, psychological, political, or economic, in which one can damage humanity, and contort its original design. In each of these cases, the agent who carries out such an action is corrupting himself, as well as harming his neighbor and his community. Of course, it is not possible here to analyze each separate action in order to give a detailed account of how each offense attacks human nature, but at least it is clear that the Council Fathers understand human nature and its dignity and integrity as the criteria for identifying certain affronts to the person.

Again, our point here is to demonstrate how pronouncements against certain kinds of actions rest on a respect for man's nature and integrity. Moral absolutes are not intended to reflect arbitrary norms imposed on the person from without, but rather reflect an insight into the meaning and purpose of man and his fulfillment. Therefore, only after an adequate analysis of the person has taken place is it possible to determine accurately whether a species of activity is detrimental to the perfection of man's nature.

The Basic Human Good of Inner Peace

Having provided an extremely rudimentary groundwork for the identification of attacks on human capacities for flourishing, we will now direct this model at the use of antidepressant medications. As just stated, the first step in the process is a relevant perception of human nature and its possibility of perfection. Here we will make use of the work of Germain Grisez and companions, who have devoted a great deal of energy to classifying different fundamental forms of human flourishing, or, as he calls them, "basic goods."[175]

Our interest lies in the good of harmony among our interior facets. Grisez at one point calls this good "self-integration": "We experience inner tension and the need to struggle for inner harmony; the good is self-integration."[176] Elsewhere we see the same good termed "inner peace": "For feelings can conflict among themselves and also can be at odds with one's judgments and choices. The harmony opposed to such inner disturbances is inner peace."[177] Regardless of the preferred term, whether self-integration, inner harmony, or inner peace, the idea itself should be plain: it is good and fulfilling for the human being when all his internal movements, faculties, and dimensions are in harmony. We are made conscious of the fulfilling character of inner harmony when we experience the displeasure of internal conflict, and the joy that is the consequence of overcoming such conflict.

This truism may initially appear somewhat obvious and trivial, but as it will become important for our later argument, it bears some exploration here, especially since inner harmony, while it is almost universally acknowledged as a desirable state, is often the subject of a wide range of disagreement and misunderstanding. For instance, one should not make the error of confusing inner harmony with a condition of pure tranquility, or untroubled complacency. A person may be quite animated and still experience inner harmony. Consider a skilled soccer player during a tournament match; all his attentions, desires, and judgments are intensely focused and working together to bring about victory for himself and his teammates. Such a state is certainly not inert, but it is integrated and in that sense peaceful and harmonious. Inner harmony, then, describes a unified person, with the appropriate concord between the diverse dimensions of the interior life.

Another misconception to be dispelled is the belief that if some course of action does not entail the pursuit of inner harmony, it should be avoided as being inauthentic or insincere. Or conversely, if some course of action manifestly promotes inner harmony it should be pursued. Thus, suppose I have wronged a friend, and justice demands that I ask his pardon.

Suppose, further, that I have real difficulty in actually feeling sorry for my action, and even still harbor feelings of resentment for this friend. I might reason to myself that I am too "conflicted" about the whole thing, and that to ask his forgiveness would not really be an authentic act, but rather insincere and hypocritical. The problem with this line of thinking is that it quickly degenerates into simply doing what one "feels like" doing, and avoiding what one does not "feel like doing." The result is that the virtues of fortitude, which propels us to do the right thing despite strong feelings against it, and of temperance, which restrains us from doing the wrong thing despite strong feelings that favor it, are forsaken and replaced with rationalizations about sincerity and authenticity.

The human capacity for inner harmony, like other forms of human fulfillment, can under certain conditions be sacrificed, in the same way that the perfection of marital love can be sacrificed for the sake of a celibate life. Here the term "sacrifice" is used to denote a kind of activity that normally excludes a certain type of flourishing. In this life one cannot perfect oneself in every way, regardless of circumstances. One must choose which avenues of fulfillment one is to pursue in both individual situations and in terms of the more general goals of life, and each of these goals and avenues inevitably involves the decision not to pursue certain other forms of fulfillment. Applied to the good of internal harmony, this means that at times we must perform certain actions, regardless of how conflicted we may feel as a consequence, for the sake of the greater good.

However, as is the case with every other personal capacity for excellence, the good of inner harmony is not to be deliberately and directly frustrated for any reason. Or, to reformulate the same principle, *it is always wrong intentionally to encourage inner conflict in the soul of the human person.* Just as innocent human life, sexual purity, the love of friendship, personal freedom, and other basic human goods or perfections are to be protected from direct violation, so, too, is the good of inner harmony.

Granted, it may seem difficult to imagine a case where inner conflict is encouraged deliberately. As I will attempt to show in the following chapter, the use of antidepressants can involve just such a decision. However, for now let us take the hypothetical case of a research psychiatrist who wishes to observe the effects of competing forces within an individual child. Toward this end, he inculcates a strong desire and a strong fear in the child for the same thing, let us say, lollypops. As a result whenever the lollypops are presented, the child becomes emotionally distraught due to the diverse urges he has been made to feel by the programming of the psychiatrist. Although such an experiment might afford valuable insights on the nature of emotional conflict, the means to this end is intrinsically evil, as it does damage to the soul of the test subject, and, therefore, cannot be condoned.

Summary

As human beings, we are to make choices that affect our own fulfillment and perfection. This is the proper goal of the moral life, and it implies that we are not to act in such ways as to attack consciously the possibilities of human flourishing, in ourselves or in others. The bringing about of such degradation is an affront to human nature and to the Creator, who made man what he is and who intends glory for him.

In order to grasp which actions are unacceptable to the moral person, one must first examine human nature to see how the excellent human is constituted, and what in turn would detract from that excellence. We observed this procedure as carried out by the magisterium, especially in its condemnation of contraceptive acts, which harm the person in his procreative and unitive capacity. Finally, in preparation for the coming chapter, we articulated the good of inner harmony as one of the basic capacities for fulfillment in man, the intentional frustration of which is immoral.

IV

FORMULATING GUIDELINES

It is a bad time for psychiatrists. Old-fashioned shrinks are out of style and generally out of work. We, who like our mentor Dr. Freud believe there is a psyche, that
it is born to trouble as the sparks fly up, that one gets at it, the root of trouble, the
soul's own secret, by venturing into the heart of darkness, which is to say, by talking and listening, mostly listening, to another troubled human for months, years
— we have been mostly superseded by brain engineers, neuropharmacologists,
chemists of the synapses. And why not? If one can prescribe a chemical and
overnight turn a haunted soul into a bustling little body, why take on such a quixotic
quest as pursuing the secret of one's very self?

— Walker Percy, *The Thanatos Syndrome*

Having outlined the Thomistic anthropology of the emotions and depression as well as the principle of integrity and the basic goodness of inner
harmony, we should now be able to combine these principles in a moral
analysis of antidepressant drug use. This analysis will assume that evidence
for a biochemical imbalance in cases of depression does not exist, since,
as the first chapter sought to demonstrate, instances of physiologically
rooted depression are conjectural and have not yet been identified.[178] It
seems to me that antidepressant drug use is not in itself intrinsically evil,
and may even be of real benefit in therapy when used in conjunction with
treatments geared more directly at the patient's mental state. However, it
is not morally permissible to use these drugs as the sole or fundamental
treatment for depression, since to do so would constitute an unnatural per-
version of the appetitive power away from the apprehensive power, and
would, therefore, involve an attack on personal integrity.

    Before proceeding to the elaboration of this thesis, we will evaluate
several common and unconvincing condemnations of antidepressant drug
use as critically described by Peter Kramer in the last chapter of *Listening
to Prozac*, in the hopes of guarding against their limitations.

Various Inadequate Objections to Antidepressants

The first claim against antidepressants holds that bearing anxiety and depression leads to the emotional growth of the individual.[179] Thus, one must suffer in order to acquire profundity, the status as an authentic aesthete. This assertion is manifested in the lives of many great artists, who draw on their sorrows and troubles, whether past or present, in order to create works of beauty. Consider, for instance, the writings of Charles Dickens, with his moving images of the plight of the poor, the horrors of prison, and the evil of child-labor, all of which he himself had experienced personally.

The fear is that widespread use of Prozac would effect a shallowness in society, stripping it of deep emotional and artistic expression. The elimination of suffering would bring about the elimination of desirable personal qualities, such as those manifested by great authors, painters, musicians. Many are concerned that the drug would compromise the individual potential for emotional and artistic excellence.

The second possible difficulty raised is based on the idea of anxiety or depression as an *adaptive trait*, one conducive to man's evolutionary success. Here we have a "discomfort as useful"[180] concept based on the model of survivability as the ultimate criterion. A person's sorrow makes him more fit and, therefore, affords him a better chance of survival. Yet this assertion raises the question, what is signified here by the term "survival"? Does it simply refer to the individual expanding his temporal life span as long as possible, or does it reference the individual's capacity to mate, care for young, and generally benefit the species as a whole? That the phenomenon of depression could be easily proved as adaptive according to these standards seems unlikely. Furthermore, most people will probably not be willing to endure their misery for the sake of propagating the species more effectively. If, however, what is meant by survivability is "holistic fulfillment and self-perfection of the human person in his nature as a body-soul composite," (which, admittedly, seems somewhat unlikely), then sociobiology and evolutionary theory in general lack the qualifications for determining what should be considered conducive to survival.

Both of the above objections also seem defective in that they appear to assert that sorrow is somehow desirable in itself, since it produces artistic and emotional excellence and increases adaptability. This might lead one to consider sorrow something to be actively sought for its own sake, which goes completely contrary to the classical presentation of the emotions in general, and sorrow in particular, as *responsive*. That is, sorrow is only of use when it is in response to something that is first presented as evil, and in responding seeks to improve the situation. After all, not all sorrow results in emotional depth or adaptability, (the ultimate example is a case of sorrow followed by suicide). Unhappiness considered in isolation from its origin (the stimulating evil) and its goal (the removal of that evil) is impotent and wasted. To encourage such sorrow is to go against its telos.

A third objection articulated by Kramer comes from the current popularly referred to as "pharmacological Calvinism." Put simply, this is the idea, however implicit, "that there is something bad per se about taking pills. Cure by the pill is seen as dehumanizing when compared to psychotherapy. . . ."[181] With pharmacological Calvinism, there is the sense that to use drugs as a solution to any problem shows a weakness, that it is the easy way out. Thus the logic goes: if someone is severely obese, he should change his lifestyle, restrict his eating. Taking diet pills, on the other hand, is equivalent to simply giving in to sloth and gluttony. By the same token, if one suffers from depression, one should try to come to understand one's feelings and struggle through them; antidepressants are seen as a cowardly escape.

It is unclear what presuppositions motivate pharmacological Calvinism. It may be that introducing synthesized chemicals into the body to treat mental disorders simply feels "inhuman" on an intuitive level. Some religions (such as Christian Science and Scientology) appear to disapprove based on doctrinal condemnations of medications in general, condemnations that are often difficult for those outside of the specific belief to appreciate. Or perhaps there is a deeper, more carefully considered justification for this phobia of drugs of which I am not presently aware.

Regardless, the fact must be stated that there is nothing intrinsically wrong with a person making use of certain chemicals for his own (authentic!) well-being, even if that chemical introduction should somehow affect man's spiritual reality. Chemical intervention, like many other physical interventions upon the person's body, is not in itself objectionable.

Finally, Kramer cites Richard Schwartz's concern over the dangers of antidepressant usage as a tool of cultural manipulation and oppression. Cultural pressure will bear down upon individuals whose emotional life is non-conforming, pushing them to take drugs against their will and/or better judgment in order to better accommodate themselves to the system.[182] A case is taken from the professional world:

> How might a substance like Prozac enter into the competitive world of American business? . . . Many top organizational and political leaders require little sleep, see crises as opportunities, let criticism roll off their backs, make decisions easily, exude confidence, and hurry through the day with energy to spare.

These qualities help people succeed in complex social and work situations. They may be considered desirable or advantageous even by those who have quite normal levels of drive and optimism. How shall we respond to the complaint that a particular executive lacks decisiveness and vigor? By prescribing Prozac?[183]

The concern, clearly, is that cultural expectations, whether explicit or implicit, will bring about abuses that force antidepressants upon those who do not need or want them. Here again, I agree with Kramer in finding this objection unsatisfactory. Of course societal pressures will result in certain misuses of the drug. At that point, our object is firstly to secure ourselves against external influences that might seek to sway us from our convictions, and secondly to make efforts at amending the culture in whatever way possible. Yet initially, we must determine what our convictions actually are regarding the matter at hand. Only when that has been accomplished can the extremes of those around us be recognized, refuted, and reformed.

In the end, none of these objections appear sufficient in themselves to pinpoint the potential for dangers in antidepressant usage, because although they are directed at certain disconcerting results of the drugs, they do not explicitly address the focal human issue, namely, whether some human good is deliberately thwarted by the use of the medication. To address the problem competently, we have next to set forth a basic principle for recognizing inappropriate use of antidepressants.

The Potential for Antidepressant Misuse: Attack on Inner Harmony

Let us now return to Peter Kramer's patient Tess, whose personal history evidently had a clear relationship to her depressed feelings. Instead of therapy, Kramer prescribed pills, and Tess appeared to respond well. The evaluative model we develop must help us discern what, if anything, is objectionable about the way such a case was handled.

The fundamental problem with this method of treatment is that the medication is used to manipulate the emotions in a way that is contrary to their intended nature, because *the emotion is no longer a response to the individual's perception of reality*. Everything confirms that Tess suffered from various debilitating emotions due to perceptions and beliefs she had formed in the course of her difficult life. The world around her presented itself as cruel and painful, and so she responded with sorrow. This is a perfectly normal and healthy response, given such an experience of life. Yet when on the drugs, and only then, she found her emotional state to be much more pleasant. It is, therefore, reasonable to suppose that her emotions were at this point responding to the chemicals in her system, not to her perception of reality. All the evidence points to her depression arising from her experiences. Then, following her medication, her emotional state altered. She was taken off the medication, and depression resumed. She went back on the pills, and the bad feelings once again disappeared. The point is that by introducing these substances into her system, Tess was, to some degree, able to manipulate her emotions chemically, and this manipulation was all the therapy she received.

This is an important event upon which to focus, for the internal functions of the cognitive powers and the appetitive powers (including the emotions) are intended to maintain a certain relationship, one to the other. As we saw in section II, the appetitive power is meant to respond to the apprehensive power. The person's emotions should respond to how the mind sees things, such is a harmonious operation of man's internal faculties. Of course, as Aquinas is quick to point out, the emotions are often, in practice, disordered and disproportionate, either because they are not properly responding to rational judgment, or because the individual's judgments themselves are disordered and disproportionate. In such cases, the goal is to achieve balance by reforming the person's judgments in accordance with reality and by aligning the emotional life to those judgments.

However, when the emotions are directly prevented from reacting to perceptive presentations and are made instead to respond to drugs, they are, at their most basic level, frustrated in their natural teleology. Emotions are movements designed to work in accordance with cognition, but in cases of antidepressant misuse, they are forced into subjection to orally consumed material elements. Cognition and emotion, instead of maintaining an appropriate unity of direction, are now at variance with one another. The mind presents the world in a negative, ultimately tragic light, and yet the individual's emotional experience is one of contentment, or even of a general cheerfulness. In scholastic language, the person apprehends evil and experiences joy.

Needless to say, this is not a state of internal harmony. For the powers of the soul to be in a condition of such discord indicates conflict within the person, whether or not the person experiences the emotional discomfort naturally associated with such conflict. To borrow from the formulation of inner tension given by Grisez, one's feelings are at odds with one's judgments. A disjunction of this kind does not merely produce conflict within the person, it is itself a form of conflict. If inner peace is a good that should not be attacked, not be deliberately infringed upon (which should be a truth immediately evident from a basic insight into human experience), then the implication regarding certain forms of antidepressant usage is very serious. Nor does it make a difference to claim antidepressants simply *moderate* an emotion, as opposed to canceling an emotion altogether, or even substituting one emotion for another. For it is the proper order of things for perception, and ideally reason, to dictate not only the kind of emotion experienced, but also the degree of that emotion. Consequently, even an attempt to chemically alter *how* depressed a patient is, without a direct reformation of the patient's cognitive evaluation to be more proportionate to reality, would pose a moral problem.

One might object that the disconnection of the emotions from the cognitive faculties is not the intended goal of the drugs; rather their use is meant to help the person feel better. Here it is important to be careful in distinguishing the intended object from the intended end. (Recall that the intended end is the ultimate state of affairs the agent desires to bring about. It is *why* the person acts. The intended object, on the contrary, is the actual course of action upon which the agent decides. It is *what* the person chooses to do.) Now, it is granted that the ultimate end of the individual prescribing or consuming the drugs is the patient's feeling better. Certainly, this is a goal of every honest psychiatrist, and it is without a doubt the desperate wish of every depressed patient. If, however, the person is aware that the feelings of depression have arisen from some conception about a specific reality or about the world as a whole (and as we have tried to show in sections I and II, all the evidence implies that this is the case), then whether he consciously reflects upon it or not, in relying solely on antidepressants he has made his intended object the detachment of the emotions from the mind through the efficacy of certain chemicals, which is equivalent to a form of internal disharmony.

We are dealing with a means-end issue. Certainly, the movement from depression to non-depression in the subject is a worthy goal, and one to be actively sought. However, if the means of obtaining this transition are equivalent to a cleavage of the soul's movements one from the other, then the course of action is not permissible, as should be clear from the principles outlined in the previous section: a) frustration of a basic human good is never permissible, even for a legitimate end; b) internal harmony between all the faculties of the soul is a basic human good; c) therefore, intentional violation of the functional integrity between powers of the soul is not morally permissible. Apply this syllogism to our own case: since using antidepressants to manipulate the emotions to no longer respond to perception is to disrupt internal unity, it should not be willed either as a means or an end.

I believe that a useful and legitimate analogy may be made here regarding the issue of contraception, upon which we have already touched. In some sense, to wrench the emotions apart from cognition is similar to divorcing man's ability for sexual, self-donative union from his power of generation. These two sets of powers were designed to operate always in unison, in order to bring about a greater perfection of the human agent, a greater likeness of him to his Creator, and a greater glory to the latter. In deliberately tearing these faculties from their counterparts, no matter what the reason, the basic structure of human nature is twisted, and the person suffers deterioration and a loss of integrity. So, to make the comparison concrete, one could compare antidepressant drugs to orthotricyclen pills (often used for birth control). Each of these medicines has the potential to be used inappropriately, in a manner that intentionally disjoins what should be united in the person. On the other hand, it is also possible to put both to good use. Orthotricyclen, for instance, is sometimes used for period regulation. (The beneficial and morally acceptable norms for antidepressant drugs will be considered later in this chapter).

Some might invoke against this thesis the principle of totality, which is sometimes used to justify the sacrifice of certain human parts, even actively (as opposed to a passive form of non-pursuit), for the greater personal good of the whole. For example, there was a story in the news some years back of a mountain climber alone in the wilderness, whose hand became inescapably pinned by a boulder. After several days of attempting to pull free, the man severed his hand to avoid impending starvation. This choice, which cost the man his hand and all the abilities and functions proper to it, undoubtedly saved his life, and therefore would most certainly be morally permissible in light of the principle of totality.[184] With regard to our subject, then, could not a divorce of the emotions from apprehension be an acceptable sacrifice for the greater benefit of the person's inner peace taken as a whole?

It is difficult to see how an attack on the meaningful structure of the emotions would be of benefit to the person as a whole. Granted that externally the patient might appear to *perform* better, in reality his internal state would suffer disintegration from the disassociation of apprehension and appetition. It does not seem that a defective emotional life will be ameliorated through the introduction of another defect. Authentic healing will take place not when the emotions are distanced from personal evaluation, but when they are reformed and reconnected to accurate judgment, and even though such inner peace and rationalized emotions are an ideal state, still we ought to work towards the ideal instead of away from it.

Proximate Effects of Antidepressant Misuse

An attack on inner harmony is the immediate effect of using drugs as the sole treatment for depression, and it alone gives rise to serious moral concerns. Yet there are also two further proximate effects of this kind of antidepressant use. Potentially both of these effects will take place, and yet it is unavoidable that at least one of them will occur. To articulate these effects, it will be necessary to recall the previously examined nature of the emotions in themselves, and specifically of sorrow. We saw that every emotion involves both a stimulus and a goal. To use the classical terminology, fear, joy, sorrow, and so on, all include an efficient cause and a final cause, and one of these is necessarily frustrated by every inappropriate application of antidepressants.

First of all, emotions originate from a stimulus, some experience or perception of reality. In the case of sorrow, the stimulating object is an evil (or, more precisely, a missing good) that is present in the subject's world. When this object is perceived as such, sorrow is the appropriate response.[185] However, what of the case in which the individual's perception is fundamentally flawed? Suppose the person's evaluation of reality is erroneous? A boy hears a sound in the woods made by the rustling of a deer, which he mistakenly takes to be a bear drawing near. Naturally, he experiences the emotion fear, which is in itself an unsuitable reaction to a deer. In the same way, a person's erroneous perceptions may bring about a state of deep dejection. To put the matter simply, someone can be depressed over a mistake. Carol Freedman makes this same point:

> Emotional problems, I've suggested, can be like suffering from false beliefs. Lucy, for example, is *wrong* to see herself as ignored and abandoned by her boyfriend just because he changes the channel on the television. And her false beliefs, we can imagine, are grounded in something like a *mistake in reasoning*. So Lucy might be right to see her father's treatment of her as a case of being ignored and abandoned. But she is mistaken to believe further that when others fail to pay her undivided attention *they* don't care for her, and that she is undeserving of the love of a good person.[186]

Very well then, supposing the depressed patient is responding to an unreasonable and basically inaccurate judgment about experience, and the sole solution offered is of a chemical nature. In this case the judgment that first caused the emotional response is never questioned, never analyzed deeply, for the displeasure that signaled the error has disappeared. So not only have the emotions been forcibly diverted from their proper function, but the intellect has also been inhibited from proceeding to a completed stage of finality, which is truth. The mistaken view of one's friends, family, the universe in general, is never reexamined. The mistake remains.

This is a most unsatisfactory state of affairs; error and ignorance are not to be covered up, but rather mended for the good of the person in question.

> When we see someone's problem as a mistake in reasoning, there is an imperative to help them understand their error. For that is the way we value our capacity as creatures who act on reasons. Valuing the fact that we act on reasons means trying to correct mistakes in reasoning with other reasons. To think it is appropriate to "cure" mistakes of reasons mechanistically is to regard our rational capacity as of little significance or importance.[187]

Man's mind was meant to know the truth; that is its good and its goal. The mind should go from ignorance (which includes error) to insight, and a major impetus for this process comes from emotional stimulation. One who is unhappy feels compelled to analyze further and more carefully his own beliefs, which can often lead to greater understanding in matters crucial to his peace and well-being (which, as we will see later, is especially pertinent in the realm of faith). On the contrary, after a dose of contentment-inducing medication, this drive can suffer a setback, and the human intellect may not attain the heights of which it is capable and for which it is designed.

It might be posed that the drugs affect not only the emotions, but also the cognitive judgments and perceptions of the subject. Thus, antidepressants cause the person to see reality differently, and the emotions respond accordingly. Were such the case, the objection we have been putting forth would lose its force; the emotions would not be responding to the drugs but to the new insights delivered by cognition, and thus the harmonious relationship between the two powers would remain undisturbed. Yet upon further reflection, it is clear that this would not solve the problem, but would merely shift it from the level of the emotions to that of the intellect. For to say that the drug is directly causing the intellect to act differently is, in effect, to admit that there is a chemical interference with the normal operation of the mind.

Nor does it make any difference that the person's convictions appear to be more balanced and accurate; if his mind is responding to chemical stimulation instead of reality, his new opinions hardly seem genuine. This is ironically expressed in the cartoon published in the *New Yorker* over a decade ago, where both Karl Marx and Friedrich Nietzsche are represented as though they were taking Prozac. The former is saying, optimistically, "Sure, Capitalism can work out its kinks!" Nietzsche, whose fervent and ideological proclamation was the death of God, is portrayed coming out of a church.[188] Granted the satirical nature of the cartoons, its signification is subtle and pointed. Not only have both philosophers had their personal convictions altered, (as opposed to experiencing a mere change of feeling), but their fictional statements while on medication may seem somewhat more balanced to us than the actual writings of either Marx or Nietzsche. Yet the viewer of the cartoon does not have the impression that a positive event has occurred. Why? Because their new opinions are not their own, but are produced by the drugs.

This last insight might receive some degree of challenge. After all, how is it possible to determine that the new, improved opinions are a direct response to the chemical stimulation? Could it not be instead that the medication facilitates an accurate perception of the world? Put differently, could not antidepressants be related to the mind as glasses to the eyes: an artificial device that allows the defective capacity to perceive better?

Certainly we must reject any suggestion that a small designer pill can directly aid the soul in its recognition and acquisition of truth. Such a suggestion would seem not to appreciate fully that the molecules of the drug belong to an utterly different domain than does the purely spiritual intellect.[189] The mind, which is ordered to the grasping of immaterial truth, is itself not a material faculty but rather spiritual, whereas the antidepressants are small capsules containing chemicals. So there is a discrepancy between the problem of cognitive error and the solution of a biochemical medication. One cannot be led to truth by taking a pill anymore than fix a car with words of encouragement.

On the other hand, due to the profound connection between the body and the soul, a defect in some part of the body (probably in the brain) might possibly preclude the full exercise of the mind. One's thoughts and emotions are less rational, for instance, when one has been deprived of sleep for several days. Or, to take a more famous and dramatic example, Phineas Gage, a railroad worker, suffered considerable brain damage when a tamping iron penetrated his skull; as a result his emotional life was severely disturbed.[190] If this were the case, if a given instance of depression or some other emotional disorder really was essentially based in biology, it is hypothetically possible that a healing action done to the body, while it would not be fixing the intellect or will per se, could at least remove any obstacles to its normal and healthy performance. So it *is* conceivable that in the case of a bodily disease, a pill could recreate the prerequisite material conditions for mental flourishing. (This would be no guarantee that mental flourishing would actually occur; only that the potential for such would have been restored). This is all very well, but it affects the present argument very little, because we are considering here patients like Tess, in whom there is no indication of something organically wrong.

It is also important to recognize that because our feelings often bear strongly upon our convictions or perceptions, antidepressants could also likely affect our judgments *indirectly*. Put simply, the drugs will alter the patient's emotions, and such an alteration will, in turn, influence the patient's evaluations. As we will see, in therapy it may be prudent to use antidepressant drugs to overcome the emotional barriers which might prevent the patient's ability to reform his beliefs and judgments. However, if an emotional state — whether under the influence of antidepressants or not — is used as the basis of an individual's judgments, then again the proper relationship between apprehension and appetite will be thwarted, since the latter is designed in such a way as to follow the former. Our convictions ought not to be based on how we feel, but rather based on an accurate perception of reality. If, therefore, emotional manipulation by antidepressants is the sole means of changing the patient's outlook on life, then clearly an authentic reform of his judgments has not occurred.

There are then two conceivable possibilities regarding the mechanism of effective antidepressant drugs as such[191]: 1) That they act in such a way as to interfere chemically with the workings of perception and/or emotion; 2) that they act upon the human body to restore the required material conditions for the healthy functioning of apprehension and appetition. The latter of these options would not be a matter of controversy, but we are here discussing only those instances where there is no evidential support that such is the case. We will, therefore, continue with the first scenario as our premise.

If, then, the perception leading to depression is fundamentally erroneous, antidepressants will check the impulse to review and ameliorate the person's assessment of the surrounding world. Such is the possible negative effect of the drugs on the origin of the emotional response. What of the end, the goal of emotional activity? Does this suffer? The teleology of the emotions is such as to stem from perception and lead to action. Therefore, if the intellect is competent in its presentation of things, the next step is to consider the will. Assuming that there really is a genuine cause for severe sorrow, namely, some real and present evil, it is clear that, if possible, something should be *done* about it. Merely to dull sensitivity to evil by chemical means is to undermine the force that might occasion a real improvement in the world and life of the person. Depression is a dissatisfaction with something inappropriate to the person, and this dissatisfaction ought to be harnessed and directed towards the removal of the offending object. "In this respect, sorrow is of use, if it be for something which ought to be avoided."[192]

This is why it is tragically counter-productive to state unequivocally that depression is "not the patient's fault," or "outside of the patient's control." Certainly this can be true in some cases, but to universalize this principle effects the separation of the person's emotional state from his own free choices (remember Aquinas's insistence on the human capacity to check and command the passions). An obvious refutation of this generalization is the phenomenon of guilt. Here we are not talking about mistaken guilt, which would fall under the heading of false perception, but rather a real awareness of some personal crime and the emotional displeasure and instability which it causes. The very possibility for authentic guilt is dependent on the existence of free will, and it is quite possible that much of modern clinical psychology rejects the former because it first rejects the latter. Regardless, it is a basic human insight that when a person knowingly commits evil, this action has repercussions in his psychic life. Two outstanding studies of this process in the world of literature are to be found in the characters of Raskolnikov[193] and MacBeth.[194] In both cases, the crime of premeditated murder leaves the perpetrator in a state of deep unhappiness, unable to take delight in anything around him. Further, this emotional anguish expresses itself in characteristically neurotic behavior. In the case of Raskolnikov, his eventual repentance leads ultimately to the healing of his emotions, (and, more importantly, to his healing with God and with the woman he loves), whereas Macbeth's obstinacy allows him no peace throughout the play.

In fact, Raskolnikov's guilty sorrow is actually most useful and beneficial to him. Indeed, to remove this pain of guilt would be to create a sociopath for whom no crime is tormenting. Authentic guilt is the sign of an active conscience, which recognizes moral evil as a present evil with regard to the agent, and an evil which ought to be avoided. Nor is guilt the only form of useful sorrow. Prolonged distress over the state of the poor, over a wrong done to an innocent party, in short, over the needs of others can mobilize an otherwise indifferent observer to lend aid. The point is that in these characters, and perhaps in real human beings, depression is really a response to the realization that something is very wrong, and demands action. An action which mends the problematic situation (as opposed to the perception) can often bring about a lessening of the patient's general unhappiness, (as well as doing him some real good!).

The proper response to a display or experience of depression is to seek the *basis* of the suffering. A great percentage of the population today honestly believes that it has found that cause, and it rejoices in the fact that the answer is so beautifully simple: a somatic problem. This unproven assumption has to a large extent diffused itself within the popular culture. It is also convenient that when questioned further about their bodily problems, the patients can resort to scientific-sounding terminology: "biochemical imbalance," "excessive serotonin reuptake," "insufficient presence of neurotransmitters in the synapse," which only the scientific can adequately explain. Patients prescribed antidepressants are never tested for any of these *body problems* (which is understandable, since such tests do not exist), and it is simply assumed that the symptoms of depression can be traced to these ambiguous physiological causes.

This sort of diagnosis is both superficial and ultimately conjectural, and it does not pay proper respect to the dignity of the person and the meaningful structure of human nature. If a person is experiencing a deep emotional ailment, then those who find themselves in the position of counselors are obliged to take it seriously, to make an effort to understand their patient, and to understand what factors are responsible for the individual's pain. It is an insult to the depressed person to give him a merely cursory consideration, and then pronounce a confident verdict, complete with Prozac. Any phenomenon is unintelligible without a well-grounded understanding of its foundation, and depression is no different. External symptoms are not enough for an adequate assessment of the human individual. Carl Elliot expresses this point rather well (albeit sardonically), in discussing how psychiatrists must take into account the holistic condition of the person with emotional problems:

> What could a psychiatrist say to the happy slave? What could he say to an alienated Sisyphus as he pushes the boulder up the mountain? That he would push the boulder more enthusiastically, more creatively, more insightfully, if he were on Prozac? . . . Sisyphus may well be happier on an antidepressant. His psychic well-being will probably be improved. Certainly he is entitled to the drug, if his managed care organization will pay for it. I only wish to point out that his predicament is not simply a matter of his internal psychic well-being. Any strategy that ignores certain larger aspects of his situation is going to sound a little hollow.[195]

The point here is simple. If Sisyphus comes into the psychiatrist's office complaining of depressed feelings, and he is prescribed a drug treatment for his biochemical imbalance, Sisyphus will be offended. He may say to the doctor, "Don't you want to know *why* I'm feeling depressed?" There is a very legitimate, non-biochemical explanation for Sisyphus's state, and the psychiatrist's facile diagnosis skirts the real issue in the life of his patient. It is slighting to the human being to dismiss his condition with a superficial analysis, and the resulting practical advice may well prove harmful.

Surely, there are times in which the person is justified in his general dissatisfaction with life. "Some situations call for depression or alienation or anxiety. Some things call for fear and trembling."[196] There is something deeply wrong with a system that views a personal crisis of this sort as symptomatic of a psychological disorder, or, even worse, a chemical imbalance. In the words of Viktor Frankl,

> A man's concern, even his despair, over the worthwhileness of life is an *existential distress* but by no means a *mental disease.* It may well be that interpreting the first in terms of the latter motivates a doctor to bury his patient's existential despair under a heap of tranquilizing drugs. It is his task, rather, to pilot the patient through his existential crises of growth and development.[197]

Sorrow, even in the form of depression, can impel the subject on to a new vision of life, a vision charged with greater significance and greater responsibility; depression can stimulate the person onward toward the enriching of his own life. If, on the other hand, the patient is advised to content himself with mere antidepressant drugs, he is hindered from that most excellent goal.

We have been trying to demonstrate the harmful effects of antidepressant drugs prescribed as the sole solution for patients with personal problems stemming from an experiential cause (granted, these causes may take a great deal of time and insight to discover; is that any excuse for not seeking them?). For when a drug wrestles the emotions away from perceptive evaluations, the introduction of a disharmony into the human being has occurred, and the integral structure of the inner workings of the soul has been violated. Further, the emotional energy geared toward the removal of some error or the bettering of some situation has now been neutralized, robbing the patient of constructive motivational force.

But what if the basis of depression, the source itself, is incurable? Suppose that there is a chronic malady, which in turn produces perpetual pain? Such a phenomenon is not uncommon in the case of the body, and in these cases it seems legitimate to simply treat the pain. The problem cannot be healed; the damage is irreversible. Nonetheless, the pain can be lessened, and there is no evident reason why the pain should not be subjected to alleviation. Continuing the analogy, what if the psychological pain of depression is a response to a problem that has no remedy? Is it not possible that depression is a reaction to an experience that is fundamentally insoluble? Maybe the patient's world really is irredeemable, and there is nothing that can be done about it. If such is really the case, and one cannot fix the underlying source of depression, at least it is possible with antidepressant drugs to diminish the suffering experienced.

At first, this explanation appears to avoid the danger of antidepressants preventing the patient's reevaluation of reality, or inhibiting the motivational force to improve the situation. There is no need for a reevaluation if the original assessment was accurate, and if the situation is, in fact, hopeless, then motivational energy to ameliorate things has lost its purpose. The function of sorrow is necessarily annulled, and one can conscientiously mitigate the psychological suffering of depression — indeed, one may very legitimately do so in order to avoid meaningless pain. Why suffer when it can neither lead to an increase in understanding or change the way things are?

Note first that this is very much an existential position. Depression is a generalized sorrow in which the world has lost its appeal, its joyful sense of goodness. To say that depression is based on an accurate perception of reality and that the state of that reality cannot be altered for the better is a radically pessimistic view of the world of human experience. It must be a harsh universe indeed if we say the best a man can hope for is that his feelings of frustration and angst be dulled. "You are right, the world around you is evil, but there is nothing you can do. Here, take this pill; then things won't bother you so much." If, on the other hand, one's worldview is more hopeful, more convinced of the ultimate goodness of reality and the potential of the person to realize that goodness in his own life, then a misuse of antidepressants will necessarily delay that realization. Recall that for Aquinas the contemplation of truth, that is, a meditation on reality, is a great assistance in assuaging sorrow. This assertion cannot but be founded on Thomas's evaluation of existence as ultimately good, and, therefore, ultimately pleasing. We will return to this point in a later chapter dealing with the dangers of antidepressant misuse from a specifically Christian point of view.

For the time being, however, we will accept the false premise that, at least for some people, experience is such that an accurate evaluation will produce depression, and that any attempt to improve these depressing circumstances would be futile. What then? Although the secondary concerns about the origin and purpose of emotion have been evaded, the central issue, that of emotional integrity in itself, remains. Antidepressant misuse, according to this pessimistic model, may not violate the efficient or the final cause, but it does attack the essential meaning of suffering. The emotions are designed to exist in harmony with the perceptive powers, regardless of external conditions. Therefore, to move the emotive life in a direction contrary to the person's apprehension, even in a context of existential hopelessness, is an injury to the integrity of the person, making it an immoral decision.

The goal of the moral life is the attainment of human excellence and fulfillment. It is the process whereby one seeks to become as good as one possibly can. It is a proper good that when a man experiences evil, he respond with sorrow. "For if he were not to be in sorrow or pain, this could only be either because he feels it not, or because he does not reckon it as something unbecoming, both of which are manifest evils. Consequently it is a condition of goodness, that, supposing an evil to be present, sorrow or pain should ensue."[198] C.S. Lewis quotes and affirms this passage from Thomas: "That is to say, if evil is present, pain at recognition of the evil, being a kind of knowledge, is relatively good; for the alternative is that the soul should be ignorant of the evil, or ignorant that the evil is contrary to its nature, 'either of which', says the philosopher, 'is manifestly bad.' And I think, though we tremble, we agree."[199]

A basic capacity and perfection of a rational nature is that it can sense when things are not as they should be, and that such a state of affairs causes that nature grief. It is an affront to the goodness of the human being to consider contentment with evil as preferable in any way or under any circumstances to dissatisfaction with evil. Undeniably, our emotions should be balanced according to a proportionate awareness of both good and evil; we are not to be always melancholy at the privations of the universe, but disordered and disproportionate sorrow must be corrected through the proper means. As Aquinas points out, proper "command" of the passions takes place by attending to the good or bad qualities of the object in question; thus for a person suffering disordered depression, a reevaluation of the world in light of its good aspect must be the ultimate goal of therapy. On the other hand, to attack a specific instance of human goodness (in this case, an emotive response to an experience of evil) is not to help the person but rather to cause him an additional harm.

A good person will never seek to make terms with evil, to pretend it does not exist, or to make himself indifferent to it. Even if (hypothetically) he should be overpowered by it, he will determine his own distinction from it by recognizing and rejecting it with every possible dimension of himself. This displeasure with evil is a critical dimension of human goodness, and, therefore, we have an ethical obligation not to dispense with it.

Although it may initially appear strange, the only reasonable conclusion to be drawn is that even if this world were corrupt and irredeemably so, it would be better for the human being to recognize that evil and to suffer on account of it, than that he be unaware of it or that he not feel it. Hence, the prohibition against using drugs as the sole remedy for depression, which divorces the emotions from our perceptive and evaluative faculties, stands. If a man sees evil in the world, he ought to be saddened by it. He ought not to avoid the sorrow with drugs.

Legitimate Uses of Antidepressant Drugs

These condemnations of antidepressant misuse are not meant to imply that it can never be morally acceptable to make use of the drugs. Even though the problem may have an experiential basis, it is sometimes prudent to have recourse to drugs in order to aid in the process of recovery. To quote from the Pontifical Council for Pastoral Assistants, "Administered for therapeutic purposes and with due respect for the person, psycho-pharmaceuticals are ethically legitimate."[200] Antidepressant use is not per se immoral, so long as it is used for therapeutic purposes, that is, for the authentic benefit of the patient. As we have seen, the patient is not benefited by using the drugs in such a way as to separate his cognitive life from his responsive life, and therefore, if the drugs are administered, it can only be ethically permissible within a framework of maintaining the harmony between the two powers.

If the origin of depression is based on experience, which in turn affects the emotions, then logically the only way to licitly alter the emotions with a drug is by addressing the problem in the patient's experience at the same time. If perception is left to itself while the feelings are manipulated in a different direction, then a moral breach has occurred. If, however, while the feelings are manipulated chemically the judgments and evaluations that led to the feelings of depression are also the subject of attentive direction, then the synergistic relationship between apprehension and appetition would persist. Thus there would be no *direct* damage to the functional integrity of the soul's operations. Even if antidepressant use accompanied by therapy still resulted in a brief disconnect between cognition and emotion, this disconnect would not be willed by the agent either as a means or an end. The agent would be acting in such a way as to maintain harmony between apprehension and appetition, regardless of whether he was perfectly successful or not. Therefore, the moral quality of the action is fundamentally different from the individual who prescribes drugs apart from therapy, thus seeking to manipulate the emotions with chemicals, independently of the patient's perceptive state. In the former case, there is no intentional violation of the good of inner peace.

It may, in fact, be prudential in some cases to use drugs in order to quell the emotions so that the root problem can be treated. Antidepressant prescriptions of this order are not entirely lacking from psychiatric practice. In exploring the proper uses of these drugs, Joseph Glenmullen describes his methods with three patients suffering with depression.[201] The first case, Jenny, involved a case of mild depression, occasioned by the breakup of a romantic relationship, whereas Lydia, a moderately depressed wife and mother, experienced depression over numerous concerns regarding the future of her family, brought on by an immanent relocation. In both cases, the patients were basically able to function despite their emotional distress, so the doctor decided to forgo medication and focus exclusively on psychotherapy. The results were extremely positive. Not only did Jenny and Lydia gain the strength and insight to face the immediate challenges in their lives, but their unhappy feelings had led to a therapeutic exploration of the roots of their depression. Through the process, which examined both unconscious emotional forces (through psychoanalysis) and certain errors and problematic thought patterns (through cognitive therapy), the two women were able to better understand themselves and their personal histories. Armed with this knowledge, they could now make certain life changes that would contribute to their greater happiness (or, in standard jargon, "psychic well-being"). Jenny, for example, was able to recognize and reform her extremely unhealthy relationship with men, which she had to some degree learned in childhood, while Lydia became more explicitly aware of insecurity rooted in the relatively humble social status of her background. Depression had served its purpose: it had pushed the sufferers to acquire more accurate perceptions and improvements of their actual situations.

The third patient, Anthony, was a much more severe case. Failing in law school, becoming physically inactive, avoiding virtually all social contact whenever possible, and indulging in increasingly heavy drinking, his position was becoming desperate. Glenmullen, sensing the need for something to alleviate the pain in order to treat the patient more effectively, prescribed low doses of an antidepressant medication. He justified his decision as follows:

> I tell patients "antidepressant" drugs are merely stimulants to jump-start them at a difficult time in their life. A stimulant would make anyone feel better in the short run unless it causes severe side effects. Therefore, if the medication worked, I told Anthony, this would not imply he was "defective" in any way, genetically

or otherwise. Medication is like a cast or crutch to aid one in healing. In and of itself, it is not a cure. Anyone depressed enough to need drugs should simultaneously be in some form of therapy to effect personal change so he or she will not become dependent on drugs for life. As part of comprehensive treatment, short-term use of drugs is reasonable if one's circumstances warrant it.[202]

Once Anthony's emotional sting had been reduced, it was possible to begin real therapy. A host of background issues revealed themselves, involving, most notably, the patient's family and their exacting stance regarding his performance and fulfillment of their expectations. Upon further examination, Anthony's highly dysfunctional familial situation was revealed. And, as therapy proceeded, he took bold measures to correct many of the unfortunate consequences that had resulted from this difficult state of affairs. Within a year Anthony had been taken off the drugs, and although continuing therapy, he was competent in the fulfillment of his academic duties, and his relationship to his family was undergoing marked progress. Glenmullen ends the account of these three patients by summing up once again his attitude to the prescription of antidepressants:

> Medication should be reserved for those patients whose depression is severe and whose ability to function has been compromised. Once functioning is re-established, the goal shifts to understanding the reasons for one's depression. Therapy — whether individual, couples, family, or group — can be a painful process, but it is the only really effective way to overcome depression.[203]

The principle, then, is that drugs may be used to dull the pain, but only in order to facilitate the treatment of the actual problem. This rule is instinctively recognizable on the level of physiology. Take the common dental practice of dulling an area of the mouth that must be subjected to temporary and painful treatment in order to heal some oral defect. Here the pain has served its appropriate function; it has brought attention to some ailment of the mouth, and has provided the sufferer with the motivational force needed to seek a remedy. However, to leave the oral pain unchecked would actually inhibit the curative process (i.e., the patient would most likely be unable to stay stationary long enough for the surgery to occur). Hence, the dulling of the pain is not contrary to its inherent teleology, as the experiential cause of the pain is receiving proper attention.

Note the difference between this approach and the one adopted in the following scenario: a patient calls upon the dentist, complaining of terrible pain on the left side of the mouth. Instead of trying to determine whether the pain has its origin in a toothache or a gum infection, or anything of the kind, the dentist simply prescribes a strong pain-killer, to be taken daily, and tells the patient that if the medication does not soothe the pain, not to worry, there are a number of other available prescriptions. Clearly, in this case the root of the pain does not receive the proper attention, and the intrinsic meaning of the pain itself is ignored.

This same abuse can and often does take place with antidepressant drugs. In fact, one indicator of the problem is those patients who receive indefinite prescriptions for antidepressants. The patients assume that this is because they suffer from an incurable biological malady, and so they will require drugs for the rest of their lives. They little consider the possibility that they have a personal problem, which has not been sought, found, or treated. Returning to the dental analogy, imagine a patient reduced to periodically consuming pills to rid himself of a chronic oral pain. His constant medication would signify that something was still wrong with his mouth. So, too, prolonged use of antidepressant drugs implies that the patient's depressed condition has been dealt with only at the superficial level, and that it is necessary to inquire after deeper problems. Consequently, the ease with which permanent prescriptions are handed out manifests an alarming disinterest with the mental health of the depressed person.

Two counter-examples will perhaps at first appear irreconcilable with what we have concluded about proper use of antidepressant drugs. The first of these is alcohol. Since alcohol, even in small doses, can have a very pronounced effect on a person's emotional state, should it be submitted to the same strict regulations as we have suggested for the drugs? Should a person be forbidden a mixed drink unless he is concurrently seeking psychological therapy, and even then only as a temporary crutch to be discontinued when he is emotionally sound? Certainly not, but then the norms articulated for antidepressant use come under suspicion. It seems we have reached a *reductio ad absurdum*, and that our earlier conclusions are in need of revision.

What this objection misses is the critical distinction between a beer or a glass of wine and an antidepressant. Specifically, in the case of the former, consumption is not necessarily motivated by a desire for mood alteration. A man may have a drink because it is tasty and refreshing, or because it helps the digestion. Or a man may have a drink because it is a popular social activity, or because he enjoys the ambiance that he associates with drinking. (Note that these last two motivations are not directly linked to the mood-altering qualities of alcohol; cigarette smokers may well start their habit for similar reasons). So even if a slight chemical disturbance of the emotions does occur in the case of all alcohol use, such a disturbance need not be the intended object of the drinker.[204] Antidepressants, on the other hand, signify for our purposes those drugs that are prescribed and taken with the specific goal of altering the individual's emotional life. The guidelines for their use must consequently differ considerably from norms for alcohol.

The second counter-example is the phenomenon of drugs used to grant some relief to bodily pain. These pain-killers are often taken independently of any effort to remove the actual cause of the pain, for example, in the case of a mild headache or a chronic and incurable malady. In such instances attending to the root problem is not necessarily obligatory, but it is, nonetheless, both acceptable and sometimes prudent simply to target the suffering. Why then, when allowances of this sort are made for physiological suffering, ought we to be stricter with regard to psychological suffering? It is hard to see what grounds there can be for condemning a treatment of depression in which antidepressants are the sole or fundamental therapy when that very approach is condoned in the case of heartburn pills.

Here, too, there is sufficient distinction to justify the disparity between acceptable treatment of physical suffering and psychological suffering. As Aquinas's treatment of the emotions demonstrates, suffering can be divided into pain, which is an alert to something amiss with the body, and sorrow, which is an alert to something wrong with the soul. This distinction grasped, it becomes evident that principles for the ethical use of drugs like aspirin cannot simply be extended to cover the use of antidepressant drugs. After all, it may be necessary to silence a cry from the body in order to focus on more pressing matters; but what legitimate reason could we offer for silencing a cry from the soul? If the soul has something wrong with it, what other concern could demand a greater right to our attention? Consuming a drug to help ignore a bodily defect may be appropriate in certain circumstances, but to manipulate chemically the person for the purpose of ignoring a spiritual defect is to evade that for which we are primarily responsible while on this earth, namely, the perfection of souls.

Summary

Based on what has been discussed thus far, I should like to offer the following guidelines for the ethical use of antidepressant drugs: Unless there is some clear evidence that the drugs are treating a verifiable biological disorder that causes depression (and any such evidence seems at present to be practically non-existent), antidepressant medications should be prescribed for depressed patients only to the extent that they facilitate treatment of the underlying psychological base of the ailment. Antidepressant use is only legitimate, therefore, when it is accompanied with therapy directed towards the spiritual dimension of the person (i.e., psychotherapy). Medication used outside of this framework, as a *sole* or *primary* treatment, violates the integral unity of the person's apprehensive and appetitive powers by disconnecting emotional activity from the perceptive experience to which it is intended to respond. In itself, this divorce will do damage to the person and, therefore, violates the natural law. The consequences of this interior disintegration are that the patient's erroneous evaluations are not reformed, and he will not be motivated by sorrow to live a better life.

V

A THOMISTIC MODEL OF PSYCHIATRY

It is reasonable to assume that psychiatrists and others who like to call themselves "mental health professionals," when in a reflective mood, must be painfully aware of the irony that there exists no truly satisfying definition of "mental health." How many of them realize that there cannot be such a definition unless the spiritual dimension were included? Yet, if serious consideration were given to the existence and role of the spiritual powers of man, the profession would possess a clearer diagnostic criterion and therapeutic goal to aid it in promoting what then would be better called "psychic wholeness."

— Conrad Baars, Introduction to *Psychic Wholeness and Healing*

So far we have given special attention to principles that should guide the psychiatric prescription of drugs for patients suffering from depression. It may be expedient at this point to examine a concrete instance of an actual psychiatric system that operates according to these norms in the prescription of antidepressant drugs. Such an example will not only clarify how the previously articulated principles can be carried out in actual practice, but will also demonstrate that these principles are in fact feasible, and when followed, extremely successful.

For several reasons, an ideal illustration may be found in the joint work of Anna A. Terruwe and Conrad W. Baars. First, their program is fundamentally based on an acceptance of Thomistic psychology, on Aquinas's taxonomy of the powers of the soul and their interrelationships. Second, in their analysis and treatment of various emotional disorders, they perceive depression not as a meaningless or biochemically based phenomenon, but as a result of the basic (and non-volitional) misapprehensions that cause the disorders. Nonetheless, they are insensitive neither to the physiological manifestations of these ailments nor to the benefits of a limited medicinal intervention in certain cases. Finally, the methods of Terruwe and Baars have produced extraordinarily positive results, even to the point that in a private audience with Terruwe, Pope Paul VI referred to her contribution as a "gift to the Church."[205]

In expounding their work, the first task must be the exploration of the two authors' appropriation and translation into more current terminology of Aquinas's psychology. It is hardly surprising that they should judge it convenient to update medieval terms like *passio*, or "concupiscible" and "irascible" in order to bring this anthropological understanding into dialogue within the contemporary arena. Nonetheless, very little of the substance of Thomas's doctrine on the human psychic condition has been altered. In fact, there are few modifications even in the realm of terminology, and since we have already discussed the Thomistic treatment on the passions/emotions,[206] we can quickly summarize the shift in Terruwe and Baars' jargon. The concupiscible appetites, which "move us to be attracted to or repelled by the known object insofar as it is good or bad, pleasing or displeasing," are termed the "pleasure appetite."[207] The irascible appetites, which move "one to seek things that are not desirable in themselves but only useful for obtaining some other pleasurable object," Terruwe and Baars label the "utility emotions."[208] "These actions are aimed at doing what is useful for the gratification of our desire to obtain something that will give us joy."[209] The authors emphasize that the utility appetite depends on the pleasure appetite, and is geared, in fact, toward its satisfaction. Consequently, the healthy development of the emotional life demands the recognition of this priority of the pleasure appetites over those of utility.

Of this latter category, the same five emotions are listed: hope, courage, fear, despair and anger. However, Terruwe and Baars place hope and courage under the heading "energy," since both are responses to a judgment of the situation as one in which the best result is tentatively anticipated. Fear and despair, on the other hand, react to a more negative assessment, and are grouped together as "fear."[210]

The Repressive Disorder

The first category of psychic disorder presented in the writings of Terruwe and Baars is the repressive disorder, which is induced by a conflict between emotions. Fundamental to the recognition of such a disorder is the conviction that the emotions are innately subject to the guidance of the intellect, or, in the words of Aquinas, "it is the nature of the sensitive appetite to follow reason."[211] From this a number of critical points follow.

First, the person is justified in refusing his emotions gratifications if those emotions are tending to an object that is, in fact, harmful to that person. "We constantly experience the arousal of sensory desires whose gratification would not be in harmony with our rational understanding of what is objectively good for us. When this happens, we must deny ourselves the gratification of such desires."[212] This is to say that it is appropriate for reason to dictate what should be pursued and avoided for the overall good of the person. Our urges are not to be the deciding factor in determining our decisions, but, as Thomas demonstrated, we are both to check and command our emotions.

Second, because it is the natural state for reason to govern the emotions, the reasonable refusal to gratify our urges will not result in an unhealthy disturbance of the person. It is instead when an appetite stimulates action independently of reason that problems arise. "On the other hand, there will be a defect in the psychic life if a sense appetite acts contrary to reason. . . . [I]t is a defect in the relationship of appetite to reason, which is experienced as a feeling of discomfort and uneasiness."[213]

Third, because the emotions are meant to follow the guidance of reason and *only* reason, when a non-intellectual force seeks to keep an emotion from attaining its intended object, instead of responding to the guidance of that force, the emotion rebels as though against an alien aggressor. The only master the passions will recognize is the intellect, and it will respond with indignation if some other force seeks to subject it. This is the process of repression.

As the utility and pleasure appetites are distinct powers, it is possible that they can come into conflict. A person can view the same object as both pleasurable and dangerous, and hence respond to it with the clashing emotions of desire and fear. These emotions will consequently war one with the other until reason asserts itself in promoting the appropriate emotion to its natural fulfillment. Thus certain states of tension and internal conflict are a normal part of the difficult decisions with which everyone is faced from time to time. Unfortunately, it may be the case that reason is not itself equipped to settle the dispute between the emotions, in which case it becomes a mere contest of strength between the two appetites: "[W]hen, as the result of faulty or misleading instructions, an individual has been led to believe that something is harmful when actually it is a concrete good for him and therefore pleasurable, then his *usefulness judgment has been formed incorrectly*, and the stage will be set for a neurotic development."[214]

Consequently, the utility appetite and the pleasure appetite conflict, with the former treating the latter as an obstacle to be overcome or avoided. Thus, the utility appetite represses the pleasure appetite in its yearning for a specific object. At this point, instead of reason controlling a certain impulse, the utility emotions attempt to restrain that impulse. Yet if the emotions are all designed to respond only to the guidance of reason, then the pleasure appetite will rebel against this coercion from the utility appetite. Accordingly, the repressed emotion is in a state of constant tension, for it can neither reach the object of attraction nor submit to this non-intellectual force that is bent on bullying it out of existence.[215]

In the meantime, reason is unable to intervene to pacify the situation, as the repressing emotion has usurped its role. In the expression of Terruwe and Baars, "the repressing emotion has been *wedged* between the repressed emotion and reason. Thus, the action of the repressed emotion remains outside the sphere of control by reason and will."[216] All the manifestations of this internal struggle, which characterize the state of the repressive disorder, are consequently not under the individual's direct rational control.

These manifestations will differ depending on which emotions are involved and on the interaction between the repressed and repressing emotions. For example, it sometimes happens that the repressed emotion makes its presence and frustration felt to a prominent degree in the disorder, while the activity of the repressing emotion is far less evident. Terruwe and Baars refer to such a case as a "hysterical neurosis."[217] At times this is visible in the repressed emotion actually overcoming its repressor, as in the case of a person's sexual urge that was the subject of intense emotional (non-intellectual) repression, and yet in spite of this repressive influence, the patient often could not avoid the practice of masturbation. She also exhibited this frustrated erotic impulse through marked flirtatious behavior and an "air of sexuality which she unconsciously radiated."[218]

With the hysterical disorder, the repressed emotion will sometimes seek more subtle outlets for its frustrated energy. Terruwe and Baars mention two cases in which this outlook took the form of a physical symptoms, specifically paralysis of the arm and of the legs. Once the psychological cause of the ailment had been submitted to psychiatric therapy, the physical manifestations, or "conversion reactions" disappeared.[219]

In contrast to the hysterical disorder is the "obsessive-compulsive neurosis," in which the activity of the repressing (utility) emotion is the more immediately discernable. This syndrome will be markedly different depending on whether the repressor is fear or energy, or a combination of both. In the case of the fear-based disorder, fear becomes the dominant personality trait of the sufferer. "One fears all sorts of things that a normal person does not even consider. One is afraid of sins when sins could not possibly have been committed. . . . One fears people, sees threats everywhere. One is afraid that nothing will be accomplished, and that everything will go wrong. . . . In short, everything is overshadowed by fear." The patient suffers from compulsive behavior, phobias, uncertainty and hesitation, outbursts of angry frustration, and ultimately depression. There are also numerous physiological symptoms which characterize this disorder. [220]

If, however, the emotion used to repress the unacceptable impulse is energy, then it is energy that will come to define the person's personality. This state offers quite a different picture from that of the fear disorder; instead of being afraid and doubtful, the person with an energy disorder displays an aggressively strong will, impetus towards achievement, eagerness to meet obstacles head-on, and so forth. Yet since the self-domination practiced by the person with an energy disorder is one of internal conflict instead of reasoned order, the effort is both unnatural and overwhelming. In fact, because the self-control is so difficult and demands all the individual's focus, he will inevitably become alienated from others and unable to relate to them. As with the fear disorder, there are many physiological symptoms that characterize this state. [221]

Understandably, these repressive states may at times be considerably complex, but they are always based on the pattern of emotional strife that precludes the appropriate cognitive intervention. For example, it is possible that an individual may develop a fear disorder, but then, responding to fear as an unacceptable personality trait, will seek in turn to repress the fear with energy. Thus the repression is two-fold: first the pleasure appetite is (in some inclination) repressed by fear; then the fear itself is repressed by energy. The result is that energy and fear fight with one another, and the patient displays an extremely conflicted combination of those symptoms proper to both the fear disorder and the energy disorder. [222]

Terruwe and Baars end their description of repressive disorder by considering a certain repressive condition that is distinct from the true disorder, whereby a healthy adult individual is placed in a position "which they feel they cannot control in a rational manner. At such a time they will assume a certain attitude by which they suppress feelings which properly ought to be expressed in some way or other, as without such communication the situation will continue unchanged." What separates this disorder from others we have considered is the fact that this repressive condition is not a fixed personality characteristic of the patient that has been ingrained and identified with the individual himself, but is rather an ad hoc response to a specific situation which presents itself as emotionally intolerable. Nonetheless, although this condition is not as severe (and is consequently referred to as "pseudoneurotic"), and is usually healed with the resolution of the concrete circumstances in question, the symptoms of the repressive pseudoneurotic often resemble to a great degree those of the genuine disorder. This is not surprising given that in both cases there is present an unhealthy repression.[223]

In terms of therapeutic measures, Terruwe and Baars are plain in their determination to rid the patients of the cause of their ailment, not simply the manifestations. "It is the task of the therapist to discover and eliminate these causes in the course of therapy."[224] Now, in the case of all these different neuroses, in order to resolve the conflicts there has to be a change in the patient's perception. Hence Terruwe and Baars discuss measures of therapy "by removing ignorance, by substituting correct insights for erroneous ones, and by helping the patient to see things in their true light and to appreciate their true value."[225] "As far as mistaken notions are concerned, he (the therapist) must assume the role of a teacher and clarify the issues to the satisfaction of the patient."[226] Clearly, Terruwe and Baars see the cognitive element as playing a critical role in the harmonization of the quarrelling impulses.

Naturally, this process will be approached differently depending upon the form of repression from which the individual is suffering. For example, in the case of a hysterical disorder, the repressed emotion (which is the more superficially apparent to others) should be brought to the patient's attention, so that he can consciously control the repressed emotion in an intelligent fashion. With the obsessive-compulsive disorder, on the contrary, the repressive element is so dominant, that to begin by pointing out the repressed emotion would result in an intensification of the repression by the repressing emotion. In such instances, the repressing emotion must become the object of awareness first, in order that it can be consciously lessened. Only then will the individual be able to address the repressed feelings.

The therapy recommended by Terruwe and Baars does not occur simply through an impersonal, propositional communication of the facts. Terruwe and Baars discuss the need for the patient to have trust in the therapist as a caring person,[227] for the therapist to be a constant source of encouragement and support.[228] They also relate the benefits of rest and relaxation (for those with an energy disorder), of catharsis,[229] and of the helpful potential of drug use during therapy.[230] With respect to this last point, the doctors believe some pharmacological intervention to be acceptable, as long as it does not obfuscate or interfere with the healing of the root problem.

> ...[T]he psychiatrist must preserve the proper balance between primary and secondary treatment methods and guard against the danger of using secondary treatments, particularly pharmacological treatment, to the exclusion, or near exclusion, of primary psychotherapy. This danger is greatest when the case load of the

psychiatrist is heaviest and time available for psychotherapy is limited. The remedy for this situation can never be more effective psychotropic drugs, for drugs themselves are never sufficient to heal disturbances caused by psychological factors.[231]

Although drugs may be a helpful tool in aiding the patient to recovery, they are not to be seen as more than an auxiliary supplement in the restorative process. Why? Because, as Terruwe and Baars point out, these ailments stem from psychological, not physical, factors. The implication is that while drugs may be of help in facilitating healing, they are not of themselves sufficiently curative. To use them in such a way as to minimize psychotherapy (even though in certain situations it may appear attractive as a time-effective technique) is to do a great disservice to the patient.

This therapy is holistic in its attempt to reform the patient's evaluation of those objects in his experience. An individual forms an erroneous judgment of sexual desire as harmful, and a disorder is produced. A child is told that anger itself is sinful, and he responds through repression. Clearly, until these judgments are exchanged with accurate perceptions, the emotional disorders will not be healed. However, to change the patient's evaluations demands much more than the mere verbal explanation of the syndrome; the patient must also be *convinced*, he must be shown that the therapist is actually correct, he must experience directly that those things that he previously feared and disdained are in themselves good and fulfilling for him. The most effective means of bringing about this shift in evaluative judgment is the prudential concern of psychotherapy. Whatever can facilitate this process, be it emotional warmth from the therapist, or hot baths, or prescription drugs, should be utilized as means for reaching this end.

Emotional Deprivation Disorder (EDD)

Another disorder identified by Terruwe and Baars is not itself a form of repression or really of any fundamental conflict between the emotions. It arises instead out of an insufficiency of received emotional affirmation during early stages of childhood development. This privation of affection results in the inhibition of the individual's emotional maturity, such that the emotional life of the patient remains stunted and undeveloped. This in turn bears disastrous results for the person's ability to deal with challenges of everyday life and distinctly impedes the capacity of interacting with others. The problem of the person with emotional deprivation disorder is consequently that of a person with the emotional characteristics of a child who lives in a grown-up world.

The potential for this disorder lies in the human being's need to be affirmed by another in his being, to believe that others consider him good, worthwhile, and lovable:

> Your affirmation, your feeling firm and strong, your possessing yourself in joy, your feeling worthwhile starts with and is dependent on another human being who: 1) *is aware of, attentive, and present to your unique goodness and worth*, separate from and prior to any good thing you may do or can do and 2) *is moved by, feels attracted to, finds delight in* your goodness and worth. . . . 3) permits his being moved by and attracted to you *to be revealed.* . . .[232]

Every person requires for his self-fulfillment and self-confidence someone to recognize and appreciate his existential value and to express that appreciation. To put it very simply, we all need to experience the sincere and unconditional love of another if we are to develop properly and according to the design of our nature. Josef Pieper writes most eloquently about this human need in the third chapter of his work *On Love*:

> What matters to us, beyond mere existence, is the explicit confirmation: It is *good* that you exist; how wonderful that you are! In other words, what we need over and above sheer existence is: to be loved by another person. . . . For a child . . . being loved by the mother is literally *the* precondition for its own thriving. . . . [M]an succeeds in fully 'existing' and feeling at home in the world only when he is 'being confirmed' by the love of another.[233]

This demand is most acute during the stages of infancy and childhood. If it is not met, the individual's emotional state cannot proceed to more mature stages. Moreover, since the emotionally deprived person continues to grow intellectually and physically, there is an imbalance between his emotional state and that of his other powers.

This disparity makes itself keenly felt through a variety of symptoms, perhaps the most prominent being a profound inability to maintain normal emotional relationships with others. The reason is that the emotional level of the person with an emotional deprivation disorder is that of a child, with an ingrained expectancy to be the constant center of other's attentions. "[T]hey *are and feel like children* in their contact with others. As far as their feelings are concerned, they are unable to step outside themselves, but instead remain self-centered and egocentric."[234] Obviously, this leads to constant frustration and pain for patients in their interpersonal encounters, as the people in their environment will naturally relate to them as to other adults, and hence will not provide them with the undivided attentiveness and concern they expect in their childish condition. Those suffering from EDD will be hurt at what they perceive to be neglect on the part of their unfeeling friends and acquaintances. The situation is worsened by the fact that normal adults often do not recognize the cause of an emotionally deprived person's difficulty, and so they become irritated and impatient with that person's characteristic self-absorption. This isolates the sufferer even more, resulting in the diminishment of his already insufficient receipt of affirmation.

In an attempt to function within society, patients with EDD will, nonetheless, be forced to form and maintain friendships. Yet since they cannot really take interest in or feel concern for the lives of others except insofar as it relates to themselves, their relationships remain strained and superficial, preserved only by conscious effort and willpower. They do not experience the pleasure and fulfillment of adult friendship, as they lack the maturity for such rapport, and yet they feel compelled to keep up appearances for practical reasons.[235] Their social lives are, therefore, on the whole extremely unsatisfying and exhausting.

Individuals suffering from this disorder also experience great insecurity and uncertainty about themselves. Because they have not been given the self-confidence that comes with loving affirmation, they constantly doubt their own self-worth and competence. In addition, they often recognize the fact that there is a genuine problem with their psychic life that really does diminish their ability to function as adults, to behave and to befriend in a mature manner. As might be expected, this recognition decreases their already low opinion of themselves.

Such insecurity comes to the fore in social interaction, which, as we have just mentioned, is a source of great sorrow to the individual with EDD. Due to over-sensitivity that comes from low self-esteem, this person will become very easily hurt by the words and deeds of others, even if such deeds and actions are completely and obviously well-intentioned. Anything interpreted as a sign of disapproval (however inaccurately or disproportionately) brings intense and prolonged personal suffering. Their derogatory view of themselves also leads them to feel as though they are too deficient to be loved, that they, in fact, are not loved by anyone. Nonetheless, those with EDD usually try with great desperation to earn the affection of others by being as pleasing as they can, avoiding anything that they fear may cause someone to like them less. Obviously, as they do not possess self-assurance, they are constantly doubting whether they are doing or saying the right things in a given situation, and expect that they are continuously losing the favor that they so urgently wish to gain. As a result of all this social anxiety, interpersonal interaction, whether on the level of acquaintance, friend, or spouse, becomes stressful and tiring.[236]

Unfortunately, although they are unaware of the cause, it is usually the case that others perceive the tension and self-focus characteristic of the person with EDD. Others, therefore, tend to avoid such individuals, which realizes the worst fear of the emotionally deprived. Thus a vicious cycle is engendered: the patient does not feel affirmed, and, therefore, he desires attention and approval. Yet his action in pursuit of this end often leads to alienation, which in turn makes the individual feel even less affirmed.

This lack of affirmation and the consequent low self-esteem impair the individual in his accurate assessment of his own person, even in very obvious cases. Terruwe and Baars describe a highly intelligent medical student who was certain of academic incompetence, as well as a strikingly beautiful young woman convinced of her own ugliness.[237] Another possible result of this self-despising is a deep-rooted sense of guilt, a feeling of personal responsibility for one's unhealthy state.[238]

The person with EDD will also suffer from severe indecisiveness. Insecurity with regard to choices is most prominent when the decision involves taking an emotional stance. For instance, in business matters, where all decisions are expected to be made "coolly" and "professionally," the individual will have less difficulty, but when a choice must be made that normally involves personal preferences and feelings, the experience is one of helpless irresolution. The person simply cannot decide which clothes to buy, or what present to give a loved one. He is so uncertain about his own feelings that he refuses to act upon them.[239]

Such is the condition of the emotional deprivation disorder. Moving on to the healing of this disorder, Terruwe and Baars are clear in the prescription of a therapy based on authentic affirmation of the person, that is, of manifesting to the patient the fact that he is loveable and is, in fact, truly loved. In other words, the therapist must attempt to complete the task that the patient's parents did not complete: the task of affirming the individual and making sure that the individual is aware of this affirmation. Therefore, in the case of EDD, it is not a question of resolving inner conflicts, but rather of making up for the lack in the individual's grounding in his own self-worth. Only when this need has been fulfilled will the conditions suffice for the patient to develop emotionally beyond the immature stage at which he has been trapped:

> ...[T]the therapist must help them experience the feelings of affection which others did not give them. . . . These therapists must

> really feel sympathetic towards their patients, and while fully respecting the therapist-patient relationship, must be able to show this sympathy in a manner which the patient can feel. The therapist must express this affection through cordiality, personal interest and concern, dedication, patience; in short, in every way in which a father and mother show love for their child.[240]

This affirmation must be both authentic (as opposed to contrived and acted out affirmation — the therapist must truly be glad and supportive of the patient; pretending will not do) and demonstrated, so that the patient is made aware of and experiences the affection directed at him. Furthermore, mere sense affection is insufficient for the recovery of the person with emotional deprivation disorder. As adults they have developed significantly and, therefore, demand a more dynamic affirmation of their being. Because the faculties of the patient have expanded since childhood, the affirmation must now expand to cover a greater area.

Patients will often feel the need to have their decisions approved by the therapist, (even to the point of showing the therapist recent clothing purchases). Fundamentally, the patient must come to realize he is loved and accepted unconditionally. Regardless of any personal defect in the patient (whether real or imagined), the therapist must convince him of his intrinsic value, as manifested by the affection the therapist feels for him.[241]

The observations that Terruwe and Baars have recorded of the therapeutic process are most fascinating, but unfortunately too many to review here in detail. Among their interesting insights are the differences between the emotional needs of men and women with EDD,[242] the maturation of their immature preferences (for example, the development of the palate),[243] and the psychosexual development of patients.[244] Throughout therapy, the aim is the thorough affirmation of the patient, always respecting the propriety of the patient-therapist relationship.

As one might expect, these deep-seated insecurities will not disappear overnight. The process of bringing the patient to emotional stability and maturity will be a long and arduous task, and will demand patience and perseverance on the part of both the therapist and the patient, as well as those people in the patient's day-to-day environment. As was already pointed out, it is often difficult to deal with individuals suffering from EDD, and this difficulty can increase throughout the course of therapy. Fortunately, when one becomes aware of the cause of the patient's problems, it becomes easier to sympathize with them and tolerate whatever nuisance they may inadvertently inflict. Even then, great love and patience will be needed.

Although this therapy of affirmation does not itself consist so much in a propositional exchange between patient and therapist as in appropriate manifestations of affection, Terruwe and Baars are clear that the therapist must lay the groundwork of affirmation therapy by explaining the patient's problem to him:

> In order to make therapy at all possible, it will always be necessary to prepare the way by providing patients with insight into their psychic condition. In practically all cases of emotional deprivation disorder, one is dealing with intellectually adult individuals who will never permit their emotional lives to evolve unless they first understand the nature of their illness and realize the necessity and reasonableness of accepting such evolution.[245]

Respect for patients' capacity to grasp the truth about themselves is, therefore, fundamental to a successful treatment. In fact, it is perhaps more precise to say that the therapy itself is nothing more than an effort to help the patients grasp the truth about themselves, specifically, that they are good and deserving of love and are loved, and that this should lead to a newfound self-confidence. It is an effort to change the patient's evaluation of reality, and more specifically, to change his evaluation of himself. This goal is in part accomplished through matter-of-fact elucidations about the anthropology of the emotions and the nature of emotional deprivation disorder. At other times what is called for is simply a kind smile, a fond gesture, or a sincere compliment. It is not enough to say the patient is loveable; it must be shown to him for him to really believe it ("You are good and loved; Look! Don't you see?"). Factual statement is complimented by direct experience. Yet in both cases the objective is to convince the patient, to alter his perspective, his outlook on what is the case. The disorder of emotional deprivation is founded on low self-esteem, ("esteem" itself is a term that connotes evaluation), and this judgment has to be reformed for the condition to ameliorate. This corresponds exactly to what has been said in earlier chapters: emotions are fundamentally reactive to presentations of reality. Therefore, to heal the emotions truly, one must correct the perceptive problem.

An Appraisal of the Work of Terruwe and Baars Relative to Depression and Antidepressants

In their work on repressive and emotional deprivation disorders, Terruwe and Baars manifest both a coherent and realistic conceptualization of the human psyche, as well as a penetrating sensitivity to incidences of emo-

tional illness. As opposed to looking at these disorders as arbitrary disturbances, they develop an intelligible account of the cause and nature of both
syndromes, so that the condition in question is understood and not merely
observed. Furthermore, Terruwe and Baars have exercised therapeutic prudence in applying these principles in practical situations, through concrete
therapy and treating the ailment at its root, in order that the curative process
might ensue. The measure of their competence is clear from the high degree
of success they have enjoyed with numerous patients.

Their expertise is realized, for instance, in the way Baars and Terruwe deal with the phenomenon of depression, which commonly accompanies the repressive and the emotional deprivation disorders. Given their
understanding of the root causes of these disorders, they are able to recognize depression as an effect and manifestation of a deeper psychological
problem. "Depression is another complaint expressed by many neurotic
persons. This is hardly surprising, for the neurotic's unfortunate tense and
anxious state deprives him of the enjoyment of most of the goods life has
to offer." [246] It is only reasonable to expect someone with severe emotional
problems to suffer greatly, which can in turn easily lead to depression. "The
feeling of not being able to face life weighs heavily upon them and leads
to an intense feeling of dejection." [247]

The proper response, then, is not simply to direct all efforts at removing the depressed feelings any more than it makes sense to swat at individual bees while ignoring the hive. Certainly, one might get rid of the
bee most bothersome at the moment, but the solution is temporary. Those
bees are coming from somewhere, and without getting at the source of the
problem, the infestation will persist. The same principle holds true for superficial psychiatric treatments, which seek only to restore the person to
an *operational* level. Terruwe and Baars roundly denounce the view that
"people are "well" as long as they are able to perform certain functions,
or hold a certain job useful to society" and that effective treatment will simply help them regain this ability to function in their given environment:

> This may be true indeed if we mean by effective psychiatric ther-
> apy merely the successful removal of the symptoms of a psy-
> chiatric condition like depression by means of drugs, electro-
> shock therapy, or any other therapeutic means. This would not
> be true, however, if we hold effective psychiatric therapy to in-
> clude also curing the underlying mental and emotional state of
> the depressed person.[248]

Superficial cures, while they may appeal to those surrounding the patient
as an easy fix to a bothersome problem, do not adequately tend to the needs

of one suffering from an internal, personal difficulty. This is a hard truth, because it means that a patient's symptoms cannot be treated in isolation, and so the therapist must try to locate and address the root of the ailment, which naturally involves a great deal more effort and involvement than prescribing a pill. Nonetheless, only by recognizing the influence of the subject's judgments and evaluations over his emotional life can treatment become really "effective." Drugs in themselves are not an adequate remedy.

Summary

The work of Terruwe and Baars embodies the principle that for a therapeutic system to be effective it must be grounded on an accurate anthropology and prudential insight into the needs of the individual. Regarding the first of these foundations, their acceptance and assimilation of the Thomistic model of the emotions provides an example of how his taxonomy need not remain a matter of abstract academics, but can be applied on the concrete level with great success. Indeed, it is a vindication of Aquinas's insights into human nature that such positive results come from putting them into practice. Without some understanding of the way the human being can function and is meant to function, there will be no standard by which to measure a patient's improvement. This is, as we have mentioned throughout, the source of many of the problems of modern psychopharmacology: *the failure to consider man holistically in his psycho-somatic unity, which has led to a technological treatment of mental disorders, with the diminishment of external symptoms as the only gauge of success.*

By contrast, Baars and Terruwe consider the human being as a creation made for happiness and self-realization, whose various facets are all meaningfully designed with a specific purpose in order to help him reach his fulfillment. More specifically, the person is a being whose drives and judgments (both physical and intellectual) are all intended to work together harmoniously. He is a being who depends on the love and affection of other people, who must be known and loved as an individual and for his own sake if he is to prosper. If any of these elements are lacking, it signals frustration, an ailment on the psychological level accompanied by deep suffering, and numerous symptomatic effects. The task of the therapist, therefore, is not to attempt a superficial concealment of the disorder in question, but to seek the real restoration of the patient's functional integrity in order that he may freely pursue his goal of human excellence.

VI

FAITH, SUFFERING AND DEPRESSION

...and I thought, How good You are. You might have killed us with happiness, but You let us be with You in pain.

— Graham Greene, *The End of the Affair*

Thus far we have attempted to examine the appropriate principles governing antidepressant use from a fundamentally natural-law perspective, that is, by looking at the person and his fulfillment apart from any supernaturally revealed anthropology. What has been stated thus far does not intrinsically require (although practically it might) acceptance of the Christian faith. The next phase of the discussion must now take place on the theological plane, for we have yet to ask about the effects of antidepressant misuse on our relationship with God.

Antidepressants define themselves in reference to a certain mode of suffering, and so just as their assessment on the natural scale demanded first an analysis of the nature and meaning of suffering, so here it is necessary first to inquire into suffering viewed in the light of divine revelation. Since the Christian belief radically defines our understanding of the human being's identity and final destiny, it is unsurprising that our conception of human misery will also undergo some transformation, which will in turn affect our moral attitude concerning its alleviation with antidepressant drugs.

Given that "grace builds on nature," we can reasonably anticipate that there will be a fair amount of similarity between the two sections. Sorrow, on the supernatural as well as the natural level, will still serve man as an indication of something amiss, whether in his apprehension or in his situation, and will provide an impetus for some kind of reforming activity. The Christian mystery, however, with its focus on the Cross and the Mystical Body, offers a previously unimaginable significance and estimation of suffering, which while not contradicting the natural purpose of affliction, goes far, far beyond it.

Reconciling Divine Goodness with the Reality of Suffering

To deal with the religious aspect of suffering is at once to provoke the classic, and perhaps most common, challenge to Christianity: If God is both good and all-powerful (as He most certainly is, according to our creed), how is it conceivable that He should allow suffering to exist at all? Would not a good God bring a halt to all the obvious pain and anguish in the world? Howard Burkle[249] offers three literary greats who, in more and less dramatic form, recount this basic problem through stirring narrative images: Dostoevsky's Ivan Karamazov attacks God's toleration of a child being torn to pieces by dogs; Dr. Rieux loses his usual spirit of resignation to protest a God who allows an innocent boy to die from a horrible sickness in Camus's *The Plague*; and in *Night*, by Elie Wiesel, an Auschwitz inmate proclaims the death of God while watching a youth being slowly and cruelly hanged. What kind of good divinity would permit such atrocities?

It is of consequence to notice that in all three of these images, those suffering are children; that is to say, they are all *innocent*. What have they done to merit such torments? Certainly, the same case is usually made for the majority of those suffering from severe depression. They are not at fault, and what possible justification can God have for letting such suffering continue?

Before engaging this question, however, I would like to attempt to make the discussion a little more precise. This problem is often called the "problem of suffering," and often the "problem of evil." For the sake of avoiding later confusion, I would like to propose that only the latter description is technically accurate. I have attempted in previous chapters to point out that suffering, which is simply a repugnance towards evil, is not itself an evil but rather a human perfection. Therefore, supposing evil to be present in the world, it is only fitting that God should endow his creatures with both an ability to perceive it and an emotional impulse to do away with it.

To give a detailed account of the innumerable and often nuanced arguments against the existence of an all-powerful, all-good God who allows evil to befall His creatures (even the innocent), and the equally innumerable responses this objection receives is obviously a task well beyond the ambitions of the present study. This notwithstanding, it is hopefully not too bold to offer a brief restatement of the standard Christian justification of the divine tolerance of evil. That justification is the doctrine of free-will.

When God created rational beings, He made them free, capable of choosing either the morally good or the morally evil. Instead of automated, pre-determined entities who would be necessarily subject to their programming, these creatures would take part in their own determination. This surely was a great good, for it is evident that a created being that can freely act for the sake of goodness is superior to a created being that has no say in the matter. Nonetheless, the good of freedom also entailed a risk, specifically, the risk of failing to act for the sake of goodness. Humans had the power of deciding whether they would expand to the limits of their potential, or whether they would contract themselves, becoming smaller and less endowed with their Creator's goodness.

> God could have made a universe peopled with marionettes, with beings that were as much mechanical expressions of his will as watches are of their watch-makers. But what he actually chose to make were human beings. And human beings were intended by God to be quite different from puppets. They were to be capable of moral achievement and of moral growth; and the necessary concomitant of this is that they had to be capable of moral failure and refusal to grow.[250]

To put it another way, when God brought free and rational creatures into existence, the distinction between "ought" and "is" was introduced. Here were beings who could fail to act as they should and could, therefore, bring about privations. If God was willing to permit the existence of free will, he necessarily had to permit the potential for evil. And it was precisely that potential for evil that human beings chose to actualize.[251]

Further, God created human beings in community. He placed them in a common world, with a common nature, in order to live in interdependence. This fact is reflected in humanity's basic orientation to society, which is most clearly exemplified in the family, a human community based on both the biological and rational aspects of the person. Once this communal aspect of humanity is granted, such that the actions of one affect the others, it is not so difficult to see that even the evil actions of one will affect the others. If you and I are placed in a relationship where I partially depend upon your good will and you partially depend upon mine (even indirectly), then it is within my power to cause you at least some damage through my own ill will. This is true whether or not you are entirely innocent. Nor is it feasible that God should prevent all actions of mine that would bring evil

upon you; for then my decisions and actions would be without consequence, rendering my freedom illusory.

> We can, perhaps, conceive of a world in which God corrected
> the results of this abuse of free will by His creatures at every
> moment: so that a wooden beam became soft as grass when it
> was used as a weapon, and the air refused to obey me if I at-
> tempted to set up in it the sound-waves that carry lies or insults.
> But such a world would be one in which wrong actions were im-
> possible, and in which, therefore, freedom of the will would be
> void.[252]

If free creatures are created in a community, then the chance necessarily
exists that evil will occur, and will even befall the innocent. Moreover, supposing the innocent to have their apprehensive and appetitive powers in
good working order, should evil in fact be present, they will feel its sting.
Bad things will happen to good people, and they will suffer. All this is allowed for the greater benefit of respecting free will and the solidarity of
human beings.

It is important to stress that this traditional explanation has constantly maintained the absolute omnipotence of divinity. God could put an
end to all evil; He chooses not to for the sake of a greater good. In fact,
God's power over evil is even expressed positively throughout the Christian
tradition. In the Old Testament, for example, we see Yahweh "actively"
punishing his people,[253] the classic example of which is the plagues of
Egypt. Nor are instances wanting in the New Testament of these supernaturally "sent" evils: to take one, Ananias and his wife Sapphira are miracu-
lously struck dead in consequence of exaggerating their monetary donation
to the early Church.

Here it is appropriate to speak about God's permissive will. All sin
has evil consequences, and God at times allows the person or persons to
experience (that is, suffer on account of) evil more or less acutely than is
commonly the case. In this sense, it is true to say that God *sends* suffering
our way for certain reasons of His own, or that God wants me to *bear with*
certain evil, but it would be a grave error to go on to infer that such suffering is not ultimately grounded in humanity's freely chosen act of sinfulness.

Such is the simple, Christian answer to the question as to why an
all-good, all-powerful God could permit evil, and consequently why even
the innocent must suffer. Interestingly, in recent decades this answer has
been received with increasing levels of dissatisfaction. The traditional answer is accused of portraying a callous divinity who possesses the power

to end all evil but refuses to exercise it. One particularly aggressive outcry comes from Dorothee Soelle. In her book *Suffering*, she begins by excoriating what she calls Christian Masochism and Theological Sadism. Although throughout the entire text Soelle avoids definitions, it appears that by the former she intends the ideal of patiently bearing suffering that is perceived as "the will of God," and by the second, any attempt to exult a God who justly determines who will suffer and who will not.[254] For Soelle, "The almighty Lord, who ordains suffering or frees one from it has in that case lost his all-surpassing significance."[255]

In her outrage against the tragic state of human affairs, Soelle has rejected the omnipotence of God, and in so doing effectively denounced the God of faith and reason. She is so revolted by the idea of divinity allowing or permissively willing the suffering of His creatures, that she would rather have no God at all. Her "God" is one of limited power, one who suffers with His creation rather than judiciously deciding when it is for the best that His creatures experience pain. This kind of reaction to the problem of human suffering is common in the domain of process theology: a denial that God possesses the perfection of omnipotence, and a depiction of God as unable to stop the suffering of creatures but instead experiences compassion alongside humanity.[256]

Really, there is no need to go about revising the classical Christian understanding of God; it simply remains for us to show that God's permissive causality of evil and suffering, both general and specific, does not entail a cold, unloving divinity. God could remove all suffering, but He does not. Why not? The basic reason, we have already stated: respect for human free will, human societal interdependence, the human powers to perceive and respond to evil, and the actual evil choices of creatures. All suffering can ultimately be traced to these principles. In fact, if we believe (as the Christian tradition does), that God has intervened on numerous occasions for the welfare of the human race — most powerfully with the Incarnation — then we can only shudder at what the universe might have looked like if its Ruler had really allowed the effect of sin to carry its uninterrupted course. Such reflections will hopefully give us some appreciation for the heinousness of sin. After all, Auschwitz happened in a redeemed world — a world where God Himself marched to the Golgotha to lessen our burden. Imagine what might have happened in an unredeemed world.

Yet now a further question is raised: granted that God sometimes intervenes, sometimes impedes the flow of evil springing from sin, we must ask, is there any criteria for when or why God chooses to do this? Or, to restate the same problem, are there any special motivations as to why God might permissively will a certain person profound suffering for a certain place and time? Are there further "benefits" to allowing evil and suffering beyond merely protecting the integrity of free will?

Indeed, there are, so many that it will be convenient to distinguish these benefits according to two classifications, the first being opportunities derived from suffering, which affect primarily the individual, and secondly those affecting the community. Of course in practice, the rationale for a given instance of human suffering remains shrouded in mystery and often confusion, as the story of Job so eloquently expresses. Still, it is not only possible but edifying to consider abstractly the manner in which God can expediently propel the person toward his fulfillment through the means of displeasure.

Before expounding on the opportunities which suffering affords, I believe it important to make a few observations on the Christian idea of suffering as punishment. This has of late become an extremely unpopular doctrine, such that Soelle goes so far as to call for its permanent abolition.[257] MacIntyre writes that the weakest argument attempting to defend God in the face of suffering is one that envisions suffering as a punishment for wickedness, which he claims to be patently false as evidenced by the disproportion between suffering and wrong-doing (most obviously in the case of children and other innocents).[258] Even Our Lord Himself, when speaking of the man born blind and a group of unfortunates killed by accident, clearly disassociates at least some suffering from personal guilt.[259]

Nonetheless, although it is not the case that all suffering involves punishment for individual sin, it does not follow that no suffering involves punishment for individual sin. Quite the contrary, on the merely human level, we commonly see suffering that is linked somehow with the punishment for a misdeed, from domestic chastisement to the penalties imposed by international courts for crimes against humanity. Such punishments are frequently considered justifiable or even necessary. When Scripture and tradition, therefore, speak of a Just Judge who absolves and condemns, it is unfitting to grow outraged, as if justice, which punishes evil and rewards good, is a virtue exclusive to humanity.

Nor does it make sense to say, "Suffering has nothing to do with God or punishment. It is true that the evil reap what they sow, but simply because such is the nature of things. We ought not to suppose God intentionally inflicts suffering upon us as punishment." If justice and punishment are due to the nature of things, to what is the nature of things due? To God, certainly. The nature of things flows from God, as an expression of His very self. Consequently, to lay the responsibility of punishment at the feet of a neutral third party we call nature is to skirt the issue. If it has been decreed that those who do evil shall suffer, then it is God who has decreed it so. "*Corresponding to the moral evil of sin is punishment,* which guarantees the moral order in the same transcendent sense in which this order is laid down by the will of the Creator and Supreme Lawgiver. . . . God is a just Judge who rewards good and punishes evil. . . ."[260]

Remember, too, that although we may be quick to point out cases of young children, who are admittedly innocent of personal guilt, this can distract from the fact that we ourselves can lay claim to no such innocence. It is well to sympathize with the sufferings of our neighbor, and to refrain from attempting to make inferences regarding his culpability; but our own guilt we know, and our pain can, therefore, legitimately take on the aspect of just punishment. According to the Christian doctrine, most of us deserve all the suffering we receive as retribution for our sins. In fact, according to the Christian doctrine, most of us deserve far worse. Paradoxically, God's punishment can and should awaken in our hearts an appreciation and appeal to his mercy, not indignation as though at wanton cruelty.

The Supernatural Benefits of Suffering from the Perspective of the Individual

The first and most basic advantage that suffering affords is the impulse to reassess not only one's own life, but the meaning of life itself. Suffering prompts a pointed reevaluation of the world. Suffering necessarily implies a problem, and it provides the sufferer with a stimulus to search out both the source and solution of the difficulty. Pain informs us that something is wrong with the world; hence, we try to learn what exactly is wrong and whether it can be made right. If the sufferer is honest and determined in his search, God may very well allow suffering as the trail which leads to His Revelation. "To this grace many saints, such as St. Francis of Assisi, St. Ignatius of Loyola and others, owe their profound conversion."[261]

For He will not refuse the answer to the question of human life to one who is really asking after it. "Seek and you shall find." The trouble is getting us to seek. Satisfaction is a poor stimulus to inquiry; the introduction of pain, on the contrary, can quickly motivate an active pursuit of truth:

> We can rest contentedly in our sins and in our stupidities; and anyone who has watched gluttons shoveling down the most exquisite foods as if they did not know what they were eating, will admit that we can ignore even pleasure. But pain insists upon being attended to. God whispers to us in our pleasures, speaks in our conscience, but shouts in our pain: it is His megaphone to rouse a deaf world.[262]

It is often commented that our age has lost the awareness of sin, and that the dominance of relativism is destroying any awareness of truth. If that is so, then it is an equally plain fact that contemporary society is free from any accusation of insensitivity to pain, both physical and psychological. This is not a generation of silent sufferers; indeed, stoicism of any kind is quite uncommon. The point is that in a culture where intellect and moral sensibility are no longer susceptible to heavenly promptings, God may deem it fitting to exploit the human capacity for suffering in order to aggravate humanity from its sloth. When we close off certain passages, we can be sure that He will not hesitate to explore other avenues by which He may extend His invitation. Nor need this suffering necessarily be dramatic; those sufferings associated with the materially well-off, such as boredom, irritation, anxiety, and depression, can be of real use if they can stimulate the beginnings of the search that will lead to God. Discontent in any form, even the most mundane, can inspire the displeased to seek some way of obtaining perfect happiness and peace.

The same inspiration holds for those who have already assented to the truths of the faith; suffering can impel the believer on towards his goal. Like unbelievers, Christians grow complacent with their various worldly pleasures and acquisitions, and although cognitively they fully accept that the ultimate end of all their efforts should be the glorification of God and union with Him in the next world, practically speaking this truth is often not borne out in their lives.

Consequently, it is sometimes the will of Providence that we be forcibly detached from worldly goods, that we may be more wholly directed toward that good that transcends this life. Detachment from a desired object entails suffering (as we saw in Aquinas's treatment, the object that determines sorrow is the absent good), and frequently intense suffering. Nonetheless, suffering that bears the fruit of detachment is a liberating suffering. Like a drug addict who has endured the agony of withdrawal, after we have undergone the divinely imposed severance from the human goal of our craving, we are enabled to live a happier, more grace-filled life.

Lewis reflects profoundly on this phenomenon of detachment with its prerequisite suffering, and notes that many times the things from which we are divinely detached are not signs of vice or even weaknesses, but are rather admirable possessions, worthy of pursuit and esteem. Familial harmony, basic financial stability, achievement in the arts, and so forth —; all of these are commendable acquisitions. Yet if they distract us from our final end, or if they lull us into a false sense of sufficiency, in the long run they hamper us in our efforts to the God who alone will grant peace, contentment, security.

Now God, who has made us, knows what we are and that our happiness lies in Him. Yet we will not seek it in Him as long as He leaves us any other resort where it can even plausibly be looked for. While what we call "our own life" remains agreeable we will not surrender it to Him. What then can God do in our interests but make "our own life" less agreeable to us, and take away the plausible source of false happiness?[263]

Thus, He forcibly removes things which we might be unwilling to give up, that in our poverty we will finally turn to Him. As Graham Greene writes in *The End of the Affair*, "You were there, teaching us to squander, like You taught the rich man, so that one day we might have nothing left except this love of You."[264] When deprived of our temporal goods, we recognize the hole those goods had superficially covered. We respond to this loss with suffering, but it is suffering that can save the soul for it prompts us to work all the harder for the only Good who can ever really fill us. As Lewis points out, it is rather disappointing that we should only turn ourselves wholly to God when all else fails us, and yet He is willing to receive us even then. "If God were proud, He would hardly have us on such terms: but He is not proud, He stoops to conquer. He will have us even though we have shown that we prefer everything else to Him, and come to Him because there is "nothing better" now to be had."[265]

Another positive dimension to suffering is its potential to purify the soul, that is, to test and strengthen the believer in his commitment to God. Although essentially the same as the benefit of detachment, testing is virtually distinct from the former in that it does not so much involve the freedom from earthly affections as the willingness to overcome obstacles and undergo tribulations for the glory of God. Just as the mind tends to differentiate between the absence of a good and the encounter of an evil, which are in reality identical, so detachment is often experienced in a manner different from purification, although both describe a process of drawing nearer to God via suffering. One further point of contrast is that detachment can occur to one who is not explicitly directed towards God, which is why detachment can serve as the occasion for a fundamental conversion experience. Testing, or purification, on the other hand, assumes that the afflicted person has already affirmed, at least ostensibly, the primacy of the faith and its dictates in his life.

That suffering can be suitably permitted as a tool of purification is a reasonably evident proposition. To follow the prescriptions of the Lord when to do so brings unmitigated joy is not difficult; but when doing His will brings suffering, then we can become sure that our motivations are unmixed with a merely human self-seeking:

> If the thing we like doing is, in fact, the thing God wants us to do, yet that is not our reason for doing it; it remains a mere happy coincidence. We cannot therefore know that we are acting at all, or primarily, for God's sake, unless the material of the action is contrary to our inclinations, or (in other words) painful, and what we cannot know that we are choosing, we cannot choose.[266]

This notion helps clarify the Old Testament narratives in which the just person is tested by God, tried by ordeal. Perhaps the best-known cases of such testing are found in the stories of Abraham, who is ordered by God to sacrifice his own son, and Job, whom God permits to lose family, material possessions, and even bodily comforts. Both Abraham and Job must undergo excruciating anguish to determine their loyalty to God. Soelle finds these stories to be thoroughly offensive, and tries to explain the former as an "archaic" depiction of a sadistic divinity,[267] a depiction to be overcome. The second she compares to a mythic account of a righteous hero overcoming the unjust abuse of a tyrant.[268] Of the latter she states: "The senselessness of the testing is clear right from the start. The God who knows everything also knows that Job is blameless (10:6f.) and doesn't need to investigate that,"[269] as though to show the sheer gratuity of the pain inflicted by divinity.

Here, as elsewhere throughout her work, Soelle has ignored or been blind to the rather transparent fact that one person can love another and yet still permit the latter to suffer if it leads to growth and strength. It moreover provides a chance for the individual to prove his love for God, to show to himself and the world the extent of his devotion. Certainly God knows the outcome of the test, but He is generous enough to let us discover that for ourselves; that is why He put us on this earth in the first place, instead of creating us directly for the celestial state or the infernal state. He allows us actually to participate in our own self-perfection, instead of dismissing our actual choices as superfluous.

> But as St. Augustine points out, whatever God knew, Abraham at any rate did not know that his obedience could endure such a command until the event taught him: and the obedience which he did not know that he would choose, he cannot be said to have chosen. The reality of Abraham's obedience was the act itself; and what God knew in knowing that Abraham 'would obey' was Abraham's actual obedience on that mountain top at that moment. To say that God 'need not have tried the experiment' is to say that because God knows the thing known by God need not exist.[270]

John Hick, who looks at the problem of suffering from the point of view of soul-making, uses the analogy of raising children. Children are beings not yet in a state of completion, of fulfilled perfection, and it is moreover the goal of parents to lead their children to maturity, to actualize the full potential of each child. Sometimes this demands that the parent challenge the child with trials, in order that he might emerge all the tougher. As Hick puts it:

> I think it is clear that [that] parent who loves his children, and wants them to become the best human beings that they are capable of becoming, does not treat pleasure as the sole and supreme value. . . . [W]e do not desire for them unalloyed pleasure at the expense of their growth in such even greater values as moral integrity, unselfishness, compassion, courage, humor, reverence for the truth, and perhaps above all the capacity for love. . . . . [I]f the development of these other values sometimes clashes with the provision of pleasure, then we are willing to have our children miss a certain amount of this, rather than fail to come to possess and to be possessed by the finer and more precious qualities that are possible to the human personality.[271]

It is the divine prerogative to exercise *tough love*, to improve his children through suffering, to "purify them with fire." Take the biblical cases considered: Abraham has solidified his faith after the trial with Isaac; Job has stood in the midst of all manner of torment, and his devotion to God is exculpated from the charge of purely mercenary motivation. It should come as no surprise that, in a world where bodily perfection is obtained only through suffering, (as any true athlete, who has undergone the physical regimen necessary to his particular sport, will unreservedly affirm), a certain degree of suffering is required for our perfection on the spiritual level as well.

A more subtle aspect of suffering's salvific dimension has to do with the fact that suffering can not only lead to, but can itself signify, moral advancement in the individual. Recall that in our treatment we have dealt with the two moments of suffering (as with all the emotions), namely, the apprehensive and the appetitive dimensions. First, the subject perceives or experiences an evil, and then the subject responds to that evil with sorrow. Given this understanding of suffering, it is reasonable to presume that with a greater heightening of the apprehensive and appetitive capacities, the potential for suffering would increase. That is to say, if one's perceptivity were to become more acute, it could more clearly discern evil, which would then broaden the propensity to suffering. By the same token, if one's emotional powers were to become invigorated with new energy, one would react to evil with an increase in force, which would dispose the person to suffer more intensely.

We can now distinguish two kinds of suffering; the first implies no perfection of the person as such (sensitivity to sin, either cognitively or emotionally, would not necessarily be increased), which we may call "morally non-indicative suffering." The second — we may term it "morally indicative suffering" — would involve just such a perfection of the powers of the soul. God could use either indicative or non-indicative suffering as opportunities of human conversion and spiritual growth, and yet the distinction is important because of the different ways in which each would be experienced. While nonindicative suffering would demand the introduction of some new evil, presumably one that could be identified with relative facility, indicative suffering would be caused by some change in the individual himself. This latter source would, quite naturally, be harder to pinpoint, and certainly much more difficult to communicate to others. One would look in vain for "events" that would account for the rise of this new pain, because the cause would not consist in an external event more or less accessible to investigation by many, but would be rather an immanent personal development. With regard to the antidepressant issue, a great temptation, as well as a great mistake, would be to conclude from the absence of any evident or verifiable explanation for the sudden onset of misery that the sorrow is inexplicable from a "cognitive" standpoint, and must, therefore, be biologically caused.

The Christian tradition offers an alternative explanation for this phenomenon: God, by a special grace, has granted the soul a greater understanding and dissatisfaction, both with its own imperfection and with the worldly realities on which it previously placed so much value. While such a grace is certainly a great gift, it almost certainly causes great sorrow, for the individual is now able to see more clearly his own sinfulness and the disparity between what he is and what he ought to be. He further realizes that this new knowledge brings with it a challenge; a challenge to forsake old ways and pursue Christ more devotedly. The tension implied in this challenge between the *old man* and the *new man* often brings with it profound suffering.

Take the classic case of Augustine of Hippo. Here is a man in his early thirties, physically healthy, well-educated, well-respected, not short of material means. He has suffered no great external evil, no bodily malady, and although both the death of his father (which does not appear to have affected him) and the death of a close friend (which, at the time, did greatly affect him) have occurred, considerable time has passed without the death

of a loved one. And then suddenly, without any new discernable evil oc-
curring, Augustine finds himself in utter misery, calling himself "[s]ick and
tormented."[272] As to the cause of this suffering, he attributes the following
source:

> But Thou, O Lord . . . didst turn me towards myself, taking me
> from behind my back, where I had placed myself while unwill-
> ing to exercise self-scrutiny; and Thou didst set me face to face
> with myself, that I might behold how foul I was, and how
> crooked and sordid, bespotted and ulcerous. And I beheld and
> loathed myself.[273]

God grants to Augustine the unpleasant grace of recognizing, more clearly
than ever before, the discrepancy between who he is and who he should
be. The immediate result is an intolerable tension between his worldly desires (in the case of Augustine, the primary impediment to his conversion
are the sexual urges to which he has become enslaved) and the call to supernatural life, which he clearly perceives and for which he ardently yearns.
The suffering consequent upon this tension is itself, therefore, a true improvement in Augustine's moral fiber, which refuses to let him rest content
with the evil in his life, and which will ultimately lead him to embrace the
faith he has so long avoided.

Nor are Augustine's experiences unique. Numerous mystics have
narrated a similar onset of suffering attendant upon the supernatural elevation of the soul. They are in fact spiritual *growing pains*, without which the
person would be unable to advance to the higher stages of union with God.
Among the mystics who describe this phenomenon, few are so detailed as
the Carmelite contemporaries, John of the Cross and Teresa of Avila. They
describe the sorrow of ascent, not only in the period prior to the acceptance
of the faith (as is the focus of the *Confessions*), but as a major theme of the
Christian's maturation and development along the path to heaven.

The *Interior Castle*, which gives an account of the diverse man-
sions through which the soul must journey in order to progress in sanctity,
repeatedly returns to the profound sufferings the soul may expect at the different spiritual stages. To take just one passage, Teresa states:

> …[T]he more they receive from our God, the greater grows their
> sorrow for sin. . . . It [the soul] is aghast at having been so bold;
> it weeps for its lack of reverence; its foolish mistakes in the past
> seem to it to have been so gross that it cannot stop grieving,
> when it remembers that it forsook so great a Majesty for things
> so base. . . I know of a person who had ceased wishing she might

> die so as to see God, but was desiring death in order that she
> might not suffer such constant distress. . . .[274]

This new awareness and discernment of one's own defects causes the person such anguish that it can even engender the desire for death. Sin and the realization of its affront against the goodness and love of God have become unbearable to the itinerant soul, and it longs desperately for some kind of escape from the torture of self-knowledge. Understandably, it is very difficult for most of us to relate to this kind of suffering, especially as there may be no evident external cause, and we might all too easily dismiss it as an unbalanced and unhealthy morbidity. Humility, on the other hand, recognizes that this species of suffering remains outside the scope of our experience, not because we are above it but rather because we have not yet reached it. In this period of spiritual suffering, the soul is undergoing not a disorder but a process of perfection.

Perhaps the most exact account of the sufferings attendant upon sanctification comes from Teresa's confrere, John of the Cross. In the pages of the *Dark Night of the Soul*, he too illustrates various stages of progression and resulting pain. For instance, in the second book, the mystic analyzes numerous trials, and for their origin points to the tension between God's grace and those things which have interfered with that union:

> ...[A]s this Divine infused contemplation has many excellences
> that are extremely good, and the soul that receives them, not
> being purged, has many miseries that are likewise extremely
> bad, hence it follows that, as two contraries cannot coexist in
> one subject — the soul — it must of necessity have pain and
> suffering, since it is the subject wherein these two contraries war
> against each other, working the one against the other....[275]

John uses the metaphor of a strong light that is a sharp pain to eyes that have become accustomed to darkness.[276] So, too, if the soul is to approach nearer and nearer to the Trinity, it will have to suffer through an acclimatization to a higher good. The sorrow endured is, in fact, the process of purification, of abandonment of all things worldly, necessary to prepare oneself for the loftiest stages of divine intimacy. The critical point is again that the suffering in this case is an effect of a supernatural elevation of the soul, whereby God draws it to Himself. Providence has forsaken external tools of formation, and has determined instead to act directly upon the soul, which upon receipt of this awesome gift must pay the price by undergoing a period of sorrow. However, no new evil has been introduced; quite the contrary, it is an improvement in the person's state that has occasioned the suffering.

How then does this understanding of suffering apply to our present object of inquiry? Suffering, whose natural significance and purpose have already been to some degree discussed, is taken up by the Christian tradition and charged with new significance and new power to propel man on toward his supernatural goal. Evil things, which in the last analysis trace their source back to human malice, are at times permitted by God to specially afflict us, in order that we might draw nearer to Him through suffering. The danger of antidepressant medications from the Christian perspective, therefore, is that misuse of the drugs could rob the person of these opportunities afforded us in times of distress.

Suffering can stimulate us to a reexamination of our lives; drugs can sedate us into implicit acceptance of the status quo. Dissatisfaction with this life can lead to the search for happiness in the next; drugs can confer contentment with our immanent world and thus rob us of the virtue of hope, whereby we yearn ardently for heaven; that is to say, antidepressants can neutralize the Augustinian restlessness of the soul that was made for God but is not yet with God. Suffering can detach us from temporal goods so that we may be open to the fullness of Divine favor, whereas drugs can themselves attempt to supplant God as the ultimate cure to our unhappiness. Suffering can test us, and purify our intention and commitment to our faith; drugs can ensure that we never feel or pursue the call to heroic sanctity. If God should desire to confer a favor of increased sensitivity to the heinousness of sin, especially our own, what the Tradition understands by "the Fear of the Lord," drugs can dull that sensitivity, such that we never experience the need to strive for perfection.

For psychiatrists to seek to relieve their patient's suffering at any cost will certainly remain a temptation, especially if the cause of the pain is not apparent. And it should be expected that souls undergoing the trials accompanying these divine favors will likely exhibit certain traits that correspond to the symptoms of *clinical* depression, that is, they will take little joy in life[277] or themselves, and they may speak of the desire to be dead so that their unhappiness may be ended, as the above passage from Teresa suggests. But as we have sought to demonstrate, it is possible that suffering arises not from an external cause but from an internal grace of the soul. Such sorrow is indicative of a spiritual change in the constitution of the person, and is not necessarily traceable by a therapist looking for natural explanations. To prescribe drugs indiscriminately to those who report such feelings may well involve medicating someone whose only complaint is being treated by the Divine Physician. Far from providing aid, the psychiatrist would be hampering the "patient" in his progress towards supernatural fulfillment. Could John of the Cross have written the *Dark Night of the Soul* on Prozac? It seems nearly certain that if he had described his experiences in present-day America, he would have been diagnosed with depression and urged to seek medical advice. Then what would have come of his desperate struggle to rid himself of worldly vices, the better to make room for God?

In summary, for a religion that holds that those who mourn are blessed, antidepressant drugs, if not carefully regulated, can pose no small obstacle to the advancement of its members. If psychopharmaceuticals are used indiscriminately in cases where a biological problem is not discernable (and, we must repeat once more, no biological problems can be shown to be responsible for depression), not only is the natural meaning of suffering thwarted, but, what is of much greater consequence, its supernatural potential is also compromised.

Let us remember that the mere experience of suffering does not in itself justify the individual or assure his furtherance on the journey to God. It can serve as an opportunity, and yes, even a gift from God, but whether it becomes wholly efficacious depends ultimately upon ourselves. Dorothee Soelle has declared that "God, whatever people make of this word, is on the side of the sufferer."[278] It is hard to know exactly what to make of this claim. Although Heaven always loves the sufferer, and perhaps in a special way, it is a severe mistake to assume that the simple fact of sorrow is enough to sanctify its subject. Suffering can incite bitterness, defiance, and escapism just as it can lead to charity, pity, conversion. Sorrow is itself only a motivational force; it provides the inclination to respond to the divine calling, but without the free cooperation of the person, this inclination remains impotent.

The misuse of antidepressant drugs falls, therefore, into the category of wrongful responses to the phenomenon of suffering. Depression can itself involve the movement of the emotions to something better and higher; to dilute or remove this movement wrongly is to be of great disservice to the patient.

The Relationship of Suffering to Christ and the Church

There is yet another aspect of suffering revealed in the Christian mystery. The mystery of the Incarnation, and especially the Passion and Death of our Savior, infuses sorrow with a still deeper significance than has been probed up till now. By His absorption and transformation of human agony at all its levels, Our Lord changes the framework within which we encounter and respond to suffering, forcing us to reposition ourselves in relation to it. Suffering is now not only an opportunity for the man who seeks union with God; for a member of Christ's Church, it has become an integral part of the mission entrusted to us. Simply put, in the present economy of salvation, suffering is the Christian's obligation.

Our Lord is Himself the supreme exemplar of this new call to suffer. Fulton Sheen has written a *Life of Christ*, the burden of which is to manifest the absolute centrality of suffering, under the motif of "the Cross," to the mission of the God-man. He sums up the work as follows:

> The point I sought to stress most clearly and most strongly was that the shadow of the Cross fell over every detail of the Life of Christ from the beginning. It fell across His Crib. . . . [I]t was the whole burden of Satan's temptation on the Mount; it was hinted in the cleansing of the Temple when He challenged His enemies to destroy the Temple of His Body on Good Friday and He would rebuild it on Easter. . . . [I]t was prophesied clearly three times as He gave details of His Death and Resurrection; it was hidden in the seven times He used the word "Hour" in contrast to "Day" which stood for His conquest of evil.[279]

In other words, there is no aspect of Our Lord's life that is not related to His destiny as the sacrificial lamb, as the willing immolation for the many. In fact, Isaiah's prophetic prefigurement of the Messiah is named "the suffering servant." Christ's identity was so tied to suffering that to try to separate the two concepts, or to promote the teachings of Jesus independently of His trails is incoherent. "If we leave the Cross out of the Life of Christ, we have nothing left, and certainly not Christianity."[280] Why so? Because the essence of the messianic mission is directed towards redemption; Jesus, as His own name signifies, had come to Earth as the Savior of the human race. And it was the providential plan that this saving action take place through suffering, through the voluntary assumption of pain that is a product of the sins of others. "Christ goes towards His passion and death with full awareness of the mission that He has to fulfill precisely in this way. Precisely *by means of this suffering* He must bring it about 'that man should not perish but have eternal life.'"[281]

Scripture is exceedingly clear that the preordained program of Heaven demanded that the Son of God endure these great trials in the accomplishment of His given task. I quote just a few passages (all of them quoted in the encyclical of our late Holy Father): "Shall I not drink the cup which the Father has given me?" (Jn 18:11), "My Father, if this cannot pass unless I drink it, your will be done" (Mt 26:42), and, perhaps most strikingly, "It was the will of the Lord to bruise Him" (Is 53:10). That suffering play an irreplaceable part in the work of the Savior is God's will; Jesus must experience suffering in all its forms, including death, if He is ultimately to triumph over it.

Such is the role played by suffering in the life of Our Lord. As His followers, Christians are, therefore, required to recognize the relevance of suffering to their efforts at imitating His example. Jesus Himself is very explicit on this point: "And he said to all, 'If any man would come after me, let him deny himself and take up his cross daily and follow me'"(Lk 9:23). We are directed to suffer willingly in communion with Christ, to join our sufferings to His. "Unless there is a Good Friday in our lives there will never be an Easter Sunday. The Cross is the condition of the empty tomb, and the crown of thorns is the preface to the halo of light."[282]

A tendency no less common than it is lethal is to anticipate a participation in Christ's glorious victory apart from a share in His agonizing sacrifice. On the contrary, the former is won through the latter, for us as for Him. The Christian soul, joined to Christ through Baptism, is privileged also to have its sufferings united to His. "Down through the centuries and generations it has been seen that *in suffering there is concealed* a particular *power that draws a person interiorly close to Christ,* a special grace."[283]

Bonded thus to the Savior, we proceed with Him through His passion, death, and resurrection. In itself, this is a staggering honor for the creature, but the Incarnational condescension goes yet further. Our Lord desires that our suffering joined to His take part in the salvific value of his own sorrows. Human pain, be it physical or spiritual, is now not only an opportunity for personal conversion, strengthening, and perfection; it is, by the simple fact of its conjunction with Christ, of great benefit to others. "Every man has *his own share in the Redemption.* Each one is also *called to share in that suffering* through which the Redemption was accomplished. . . . . Thus each man, in his suffering, can also become a sharer in the redemptive suffering of Christ."[284]

God has graciously decreed that the followers of Christ should be empowered to use their own sufferings for the good of the human family. Our Lord's saving action at Calvary, while perfect in itself, was nonetheless left purposefully unfinished, for He willed that we ourselves fulfill what He began during His earthly life. St. Paul makes precisely this point in his letter to the Colossians: "Now I rejoice in my sufferings for your sake, and in my flesh *I complete what is lacking in Christ's afflictions* for the sake of his body, that is, the Church" (1:24). What yet remains to be completed in Christ's afflictions? Very plainly, it remains for us to suffer with Him. He has done His part, and He awaits our response, a response which will enable us to be co-sufferers and co-redeemers. There is much to be suffered by the members of the Church before our own part in the saving of souls is accomplished.

In the passage just quoted from Colossians 1, St. Paul brings attention to the duty of Christians towards Christ's body, which is the Church. Just as in Baptism the person is joined to Our Lord, so, too, he is made a member of the One, Holy, Catholic, and Apostolic Church. The Christian belongs to the bride as well as to the bridegroom. Indeed, the two cannot be separated; Our Lord Himself goes so far as to identify them to Saul on the road to Damascus (Acts 9:4,5). Necessarily then, the Christian vocation to suffering must be contextualized within an understanding of the relation of the individual to the Church.

St. Paul's analogy of a body is most helpful here, an image of which Pius XII takes full advantage. In his encyclical *Mystici Corporis Christi* the Pontiff states:

> But a body calls also for a multiplicity of members, which are linked together in such a way as to help one another. . . . So in the Church the individual members do not live for themselves alone, but also help their fellows, and all work in mutual collaboration for the common comfort and for the more perfect building up of the whole Body.[285]

Each Christian is obliged to devote himself to the service of the Church and the members thereof. The divine economy in which we find ourselves is not limited to the individual's relationship with God; we must also tend to our neighbors, and to the Church as a whole. Practically, this service includes a willingness to suffer for their sakes, as did Our Lord on the Cross. "Let them all remember that their sufferings are not in vain, but that they will turn to their own immense gain and that of the Church, if to this end they bear them with patience."[286]

This honor brings with it a massive responsibility. If God has intentionally left the work of redemption "incomplete," then without the proper human response it will remain incomplete. "This is a deep mystery, and an inexhaustible subject of meditation, that the salvation of many depends on the prayers and voluntary penances which the members of the Mystical Body of Jesus Christ offer for this intention. . . ."[287] The way in which we respond to our suffering will to some degree determine the effect had on humanity by the Crucifixion of the Redeemer. "These heavenly gifts will surely flow more abundantly . . . if we restrain this mortal body by voluntary mortification, denying it what is forbidden, and by forcing it to do what is hard and distasteful; and finally, if we humbly accept as from God's hands the burdens and sorrows of this present life."[288] It is difficult to exaggerate the importance of the significance which Providence has attached to our suffering.

Although *Mystici Corporis* applauds the practice of voluntary penance, this teaching should not be misunderstood as to imply that the faithful Christian is prohibited from all conscious evasion of personal suffering. Life according to such a standard is entirely unrealistic. Still, the doctrine of the potentially redemptive value of human misery does provide principles for the proper understanding and response to the sorrow for which we can find no morally acceptable remedy. On an objective scale, there is no higher compensation that can be offered for our pain than the knowledge that, if we choose to unite it to Christ's on the cross, it will bring us and our fellow souls closer to God.

Summary

Why such focus on the relationship between suffering, God, Christ, and the Church? Does our inquiry really demand the rehearsal of these regularly repeated themes? I think perhaps it does. For the antidepressant culture, or "era" as Healy calls it, is a phenomenon that is, to a large degree, the product of a general misunderstanding, or more precisely non-awareness of the meaning and significance of suffering. Just as contemporary society often sees pleasure as the ultimate good, so pain is in itself regarded as the ultimate evil, to be eliminated in whatever manner possible. Depression, therefore, as a specific form of human misery, has become a primary target in the cultural war against suffering. To counter this (very understandable!) prejudice against suffering, it is absolutely essential to highlight its beneficial aspect. Only then will the harmful effects wrought by inappropriate or indiscriminate antidepressant prescriptions become apparent.

The natural teleology of suffering has already been explored in earlier chapters, but it is impossible to understand the full damage done by antidepressant misuse without the realization of the efficacy of suffering within God's salvific plan. Heaven permits suffering, not only as an inevitable consequence of sin and a just punishment for transgressions, but as a stimulus for conversion, a tool for detachment and purification, a test of the person's love and commitment to God. Suffering itself can be a supernatural gift of sensitivity to and movement against the heinousness of moral evil. Accordingly, when suffering is treated as a biochemical disorder to be dealt with merely through pills, not only is the integrity of the person violated, but these various latent spiritual advantages are discarded. The potential supernatural goods linked to suffering can thus become privations through an improper use of drugs.

But the greatest profit attached to suffering through divine providence is the victim's option to offer up his pain to Christ, thus becoming a co-redeemer with and under him. This is the astonishing fact of which our faith assures us:

> Christ does not explain in the abstract the reasons for suffering, but before all else He says: "Follow me!" Come! Take part through your suffering in this work of saving the world, a salvation achieved through my suffering! Through my cross! Gradually, *as the individual takes up his cross*, spiritually uniting himself to the cross of Christ, the salvific meaning of suffering is revealed before him.[289]

Once the Christian world recalls this fundamental reality, it will perhaps proceed with greater caution when dealing with the emotional experience upon which may depend the eternal destiny of souls.

CONCLUSION

In a world rapidly changing, both scientifically and culturally, it is the obligation of those possessed of the truths and heritage of the Catholic faith to reflect upon them, and to make use of that reflection in responding to modern issues. The case of antidepressants is especially pressing, as it regards the psychological management of many millions of people worldwide, impacting human lives at a most intimate level. Yet as we have noted, the contemporary understanding (or lack thereof) of the human being as well as popular misconceptions about the relation of biology and drugs to depression leave secular society ill-equipped to address the question of how and when these drugs are to be used, and what personal consequences may be anticipated if the medications are misused.

From classic Catholic anthropology and moral thought, specific principles emerge that enable the formulation of precepts governing how drugs directed at depression are to be prescribed. Looking first at Aquinas's taxonomy of the emotions — specifically sorrow (of which depression is a consequence) — we see the definite relationship between emotion and apprehension/evaluation, as well as the meaningful structure of sorrow as a reaction to evil and a stimulus to ameliorate the state in which one finds oneself. This conceptual schema of the emotions, tied to the moral principles concerning the safeguarding of basic human integrity, specifically the good of internal harmony, yields the fundamental rule for antidepressant drugs, namely, *that one may not directly and intentionally use chemical means to disconnect the appetitive powers from the apprehensive powers*, as they are meant to work in concord, with the former responding to the latter's presentation of reality. If this rule is broken, it will constitute a compromise of human goodness and is rightly considered a moral evil. Furthermore, such an attack will frustrate the natural benefits of sorrow, that is, the improvement of one's perception of life or the improvement of life itself.

This is not to say that antidepressants can never be morally permissible; making use of these drugs to alleviate feelings of depression is not in itself an intrinsically evil act. On the contrary, if prescribed with the conscious resolve to protect the synergy between perception and the emotions, antidepressants can greatly advance the therapeutic process. Practically speaking, this resolve means that one must not use drugs as the fundamental or sole solution to the problem of depression. Antidepressants are rather a secondary tool for facilitating the curative process by confronting the true source of the patient's condition. Chemical intervention may in certain cases be prudent; it itself is not to be identified with the end.

As a testimony to the practicability of employing these principles, the clinical psychiatry of Conrad Baars and Anna Terruwe is a fine example. Their intelligible adaptation of Aquinas's psychology provides a context within which to understand the origin and appropriate remedial treatment of their patients' disorders (notably the repressive disorder and the emotional deprivation disorder) and associated symptoms, one of which is depression. The therapeutic recommendations of Terruwe and Baars take into account the beneficial character of pharmaceuticals, provided they are used as a supplement and not a substitute for the authentic healing that must take place at the psychological level. Symptom reduction is insufficient; the ailment can only be overcome if the therapist seeks to understand and attend to the underlying cause.

Finally, from the perspective of faith, the supernatural value of suffering, which is of course inclusive of depression, grants a new awareness of the loss incurred by wrongfully avoiding the sorrows to which we are called. God may send suffering to prompt us onwards towards conversion, repentance, detachment, courage, purification, and a share in His Son's redemptive mission. An unethical drugging of the emotions is dangerous not only to our natural state, but can also impede our own spiritual sanctification and that of the Church and the world.

These are the guidelines that ought to regulate the promotion and consumption of antidepressant drugs. How they are best promulgated and implemented is a much broader question on the practical level. What is clear is the need for members of society, and especially those professionals working in the domain of mental health, to realize the importance and meaning of the emotions, and to reject the culture of complacency that advocates the categorical elimination of suffering by whatever means possible. Only then will an individual's feelings be seen as an aid to his fulfillment, carrying him towards goodness and away from evil. Of course we ought not to expect a grand-scale public epiphany on the intelligibility and proper guidance of the emotions in the near future. Nonetheless, a reform in the way people view and respond to depression will be a good beginning.

NOTES

¹ *Better Than Well: American Science Meets the American Dream* (New York: W. W. Norton & Company, 2003), 123. Robert M. Sapolsky also predicts that rates of depression will only rise in the foreseeable future: "Will We Still Be Sad Fifty Years from Now?" in *The Next Fifty Years: Science in the First Half of the Twenty-First Century*, ed., John Brockman, (New York: Vintage Books, 2002), 105–113.

² Alasdair MacIntyre describes the character of the modern therapist as one who "treats ends as given, as outside his scope; his concern is with technique, with effectiveness in transforming neurotic symptoms into directed energy, maladjusted individuals into well-adjusted ones . . . truth has been displaced as a value and replaced by psychological effectiveness." *After Virtue* (Notre Dame, IN: University of Notre Dame Press, 1981), 30.

³ The modern psychological sciences have especially neglected the person's relationship to God into their various systems. As Gladys Sweeney accurately sums up, psychology in general "posits a truncated view of man, one that fails to incorporate his spiritual side, his desire for transcendence. It refuses to acknowledge his powerful yearning for the love of God and the corresponding desire to love and give of himself to other human beings." *Human Nature in Its Wholeness: A Roman Catholic Perspective*, ed. Daniel N. Robinson, Gladys M. Sweeney, and Richard Gill , L.C., (Washington, D.C.: The Catholic University of America Press, 2006), 2.

⁴ Elliot, *Better Than Well*, 51.

⁵ For accounts of the physical side-effects normally associated with each antidepressant, see Carol Turkington and Eliot F. Kaplan, *Making the Antidepressant Decision: How to Choose the Right Treatment Option for You or Your Loved One* (Chicago: Contemporary Books, 2001). For discussions of the more vivid personality disturbances resulting from the drugs with regard to emotional blunting and emotional over-stimulation, (whether side-effects or simply cases of excessive efficiency) see Elliot, *Better Than Well*, 73–75; Joseph Glenmullen, *Prozac Backlash: Overcoming the Dangers of Prozac, Zoloft, Paxil, and Other Antidepressants with Safe, Effective Alternatives* (New York: Simon & Schuster, 2000); Peter R. Breggin, *The Antidepressant Fact Book: What Your Doctor Won't Tell You About Prozac, Zoloft, Paxil, Celexa, and Luvox* (Cambridge: Perseus Publishing, 2001).

⁶ Harold Walach and Irving Kirsch, "Herbal Treatments and Antidepressant Medication," in *Science and Pseudoscience in Clinical Psychology*, eds. Scott O. Lilienfeld, Steven Jay Lynn, Jeffrey M. Lohr (New York: The Guilford Press, 2003), 306–325, 306. For updated statistics on depression, c.f., The National In-

stitute of Mental Health, *The Numbers Count: Mental Disorders in America*, http://www.nimh.nih.gov/publicat/numbers.cfm, date last accessed 3/13/2007. For a technical analysis of the damage done to economic productivity of depression, c.f., Paul E. Greenberg, Ronald C. Kessler, Tara L. Nells, Stan N. Finkelstein and Erst R. Berndt, "Depression in the Workplace: An Economic Perspective," in *Selective Serotonin Re-uptake Inhibitors*, 2nd ed., ed. J.P. Feighner and W.F. Boyer, (Chichester: John Wiley & Sons, 1996), 327–63.

[7] *The Science of Happiness: How Our Brains Make Us Happy — And What We Can Do to Get Happier*, trans. Stephen Lehmann, (New York: Marlowe & Company, 2002), xvii.

[8] Walach and Kirsch, "Herbal Treatments," 306.

[9] E. Siobahn Mitchell, *Antidepressants* (Philadelphia: Chelsea House Publishers, 2004), 8–10.

[10] As I am not myself a trained professional in the fields of neurochemistry or mental health, I will, of course, be relying on the testimony of experts in those fields.

[11] *Essential Guide to Depression*, (New York: Pocket Books, 1998), 5–6.

[12] Ibid., 22–36.

[13] Ibid., 36–57.

[14] Ibid., 58, 83, 145.

[15] Ibid., 176–185.

[16] C.f., Eric J. Nestler, Michel Barrot, Jalph J. DiLeone, Amelia J. Eisch, Stephen J. Gold, and Lisa M. Monteggia, "Neurobiology of Depression," *Neuron* 28 (2002): 13–25.

[17] *Essential Guide to Depression.*, 59–83, 145.

[18] *Depressive Disorders*, 2nd ed., ed. Mario Maj and Norman Sartorious, (West Sussex: John Wiley and Sons, 2002), 5.

[19] Peter R. Breggin, *The Antidepressant Fact Book:* 21. For further discussion on the relationship between antidepressant medications and the common conception of depression, see pages 23–25.

[20] The following history is taken primarily from David Healy, *The Antidepressant Era* (Cambridge: Harvard University Press, 1997), chapters 2, 5.

[21] Preface to *Antidepressants: Past, Present, Future*, ed. Sheldon H. Preskorn, John P. Feighner, Christina Y. Stanga, Ruth Ross (New York: Springer, 2004).

[22] Healy, *Antidepressant Era*, 143.

[23] Ibid., 145–147.

[24] J. Axelrod, R. Whitby and G. Hertting, "Effect of Psychotropic Drugs on the Uptake of Tritiated Noradrenaline by Tissues," *Science* 133 (1961): 383–384.

[25] Mitchell, *Antidepressants*, 19.

[26] Ibid., 8.

[27] *The Science of Happiness: Unlocking the Mysteries of Mood*, (NY: John Wiley & Sons, 2000), 62.

[28] Healy, *Antidepressant Era*, 164, 176.

[29] Carol Turkington and Eliot F. Kaplan, *Making the Antidepressant Decision: How to Choose the Right Treatment Option for You or Your Loved One* (Chicago: Contemporary Books, 2001), 184.

[30] Turkington and Kaplan, *Making the Antidepressant Decision*, 187.

[31] Peter Breggin, *Toxic Psychiatry: Why Therapy, Empathy, and Love Must Replace the Drugs, Electroshock, and Biochemical Theories of the "New Psychiatry,"* (NY: St. Martin's Press, 1991), 173–179.

[32] Breggin, *Toxic Psychiatry*, 173.

[33] Turkington and Kaplan, *Making the Antidepressant Decision*, 47.

[34] Ibid.

[35] As quoted by Breggin, *Toxic Psychiatry*, 198. C.f., Max Fink, *Convulsive Therapy: Theory and Practice* (NY: Raven), 1973.

[36] Ibid.

[37] Healy, *Antidepressant Era*, 169.

[38] Certain researches hope to find the mechanism of treatments like lithium and ECT in their effects on intracellular signaling pathways. C.f., Joseph T. Coyle and Ronald S. Duman, "Finding the Intracellular Signaling Pathways Affected by Mood Disorder Treatments," *Neuron* 38 (2003): 157–160.

[39] Glenmullen, *Prozac Backlash*, 193.

[40] In *From Placebo to Panacea: Putting Psychiatric Drugs to the Test*, eds. Seymour Fisher and Roger P. Greenberg (New York: John Wiley & Sons, Inc., 1997), 116.

[41] The President's Council on Bioethics, *Beyond Therapy: Biotechnology and the Pursuit of Happiness*, 238, http://www.bioethics.gov/reports/beyondtherapy/beyond_therapy_final_webcorrected.pdf, date last accessed 3/16/2007.

[42] Breggin, *Antidepressant Fact Book*, 22.

[43] "Biological Markers of Depression," in *Antidepressants: Past, Present, and Future*, eds. Sheldon H. Preskorn, John P. Geighner, Christina Y. Stanga, and Ruth Ross (NY: Springer, 2004), 118.

[44] Ibid., 121.

[45] Ibid., 138.

[46] See, for instance, William S. Appleton, *The New Antidepressants and Antianxieties: What You Need to Know about Zoloft, Paxil, Wellbutrin, Effexor, Clonazepam, Ambien, and More,* (NY: Plume, 2004), 28–31, AMA, *Essential Guide*, 58–99.

[47] Breggin, *The Antidepressant Fact Book*, 21.

[48] "Biochemical and Physiological Processes in Brain Function and Drug Actions," in *Antidepressants: Past, Present, and Future*, 4.

[49] John P. Hewitt, Michael R. Fraser, and Leslie Beth Berger, "Is It Me or Is It Prozac? Antidepressants and the Construction of Self," in *Pathology and the Postmodern: Mental Illness as Discourse and Experience*, ed. Dwight Fee (London: Sage Publications, 2000), 164.

[50] Ramon Trullas, "Functional NMDA Antagonists: A New Class of Antidepressant Agents," in *Antidepressants: New Pharmacological Strategies*, ed. Phil Skolnick, (Totowa: Humana Press, 1997), 103.

[51] As quoted by Turkington and Kaplan, *Making the Antidepressant Decision*, 56.

[52] *Better Than Well,* 125. Cf. David Healy, *Let Them Eat Prozac: The Unhealthy Relationship between the Pharmaceutical Industry and Depression*, New York:

New York University Press, 2004).

[53] S. H. Preskorn, R. Ross, "Overview of Currently Available Antidepressants," in *Antidepressants: Past, Present, and Future*, 178.

[54] Glenmullen, *Prozac Backlash*, 193.

[55] Breggin, *The Antidepressant Fact Book*, 24.

[56] Healy, *Antidepressant Era*, 161.

[57] Glenmullen, *Prozac Backlash*, 198.

[58] James Morrison, *Straight Talk about Your Mental Health* (NY: The Guilford Press), 2002.

[59] Terry Lynch, *Beyond Prozac: Healing Mental Suffering without Drugs* (Dublin: Marino Books, 2001), 115.

[60] Ibid., 115–116.

[61] Breggin, *Toxic Psychiatry*, 134–135.

[62] We see in the story of Mrs. Pulsky a helpful illustration of the different causes as related to depression: the efficient cause (her husband's abusive action, the original source of the problem), the formal cause (the psychological damage she underwent), and the material cause (the sensibly discernable characteristics). We will speak of the final cause of depression in the following chapters.

[63] Hewitt, Fraser, and Berger, "Is It Me or Is It Prozac?" 175.

[64] Ibid. For further testimony from antidepressant users on the confused sense of identity, c.f., David A. Karp, *Is It Me or My Meds? Living with Antidepressants*, (Cambridge: Harvard University Press, 2006), especially 95–126.

[65] Peter D. Kramer, *Listening to Prozac* (NY: Viking, 1993), 13.

[66] Ibid., 1–2.

[67] Ibid., 4, 7.

[68] Ibid., 1–13.

[69] Ibid., 19. For an analysis of SSRI personality and behavior modifications on nondepressed patients, c.f., Brian Knutson, et al, "Selective Alteration of Personality and Social Behavior by Serotonergic Intervention," *The American Journal of Psychiatry* 155 (1998): 373–379 and Catherine J Harmer, Simon A Hill, Matthew J Taylor, Philip J Cowen, Guy M Goodwin, "Toward a Neuropsychological Theory of Antidepressant Drug Action: Increase in Positive Emotional Bias after Potentiation of Norepinephrine Activity," *The American Journal of Psychiatry* 160 (2003): 990–92.

[70] Ibid., 10. For an account of a remarkably similar clinical use of Prozac, c.f., Samuel H. Barondes, *Better Than Prozac: Creating the Next Generation of Psychiatric Drugs,* (NY: Oxford University Press, 2005), 3–16.

[71] Ibid., 15, 20.

[72] American Psychiatric Association, *Diagnostic and Statistical Manual of Mental Disorders*, 4th ed., (Washington, DC: American Psychiatric Association, 2000), 356.

[73] Breggin, *The Antidepressant Fact Book*: 20

[74] Ibid., 352.

[75] Shawn D. Floyd, "Aquinas on Emotion: A Response to Some Recent Interpretations," *History of Philosophy Quarterly*, 15 (1998):161–175, 164.

[76] *ST*, I–II, Q. 23, a. 4.

[77] Ibid.

[78] Simo Knuuttila, *Emotions in Ancient and Medieval Philosophy* (Oxford: Clarendon Press, 2004), 243.

[79] *ST*, Q. 23, art. 2.

[80] Ibid, Q. 23, art. 3.

[81] Peter King, "Aquinas on the Passions," in *Thomas Aquinas: Contemporary Philosophical Perspectives,* ed. Brian Davies (NY: Oxford University Press, 2002), 353–384, 361.

[82] Mark P. Drost, "Intentionality in Aquinas' Theory of Emotions," *International Philosophical Quarterly* 31 (1991): 449–460, 451.

[83] Claudia Eisen Murphy, "Aquinas on Our Responsibility for Our Emotions," *Medieval Philosophy and Theology* 8 (1999): 163–205, 167, 168.

[84] G. Simon Harak, *Virtuous Passions: The Formation of Christian Character*, (Mahwah: Paulist Press, 1993), 1.

[85] *ST*, I, Q. 81, a. 3, ad. 2.

[86] C.f. on this point Richard Sorabji, *Emotion and Peace of Mind: From Stoic Agitation to Christian Temptation* (Oxford: Oxford University Press, 2000), esp. chapters 3 and 22 on "first movements."

[87] *ST*, I–II, Q. 22, a. 2.

[88] Ibid., I, Q. 80, a. 2.

[89] Ibid., I–II, Q. 22, a. 1.

[90] Ibid., I–II, Q. 24, a. 1, ad. 1. For a comparison of the passions of animals and humans, see Stephen Loughlin, "Similarities and Differences Between Human and Animal Emotion in Aquinas's Thought," *The Thomist* 65 (2001): 45–65.

[91] *ST*, I–II, Q. 22, a. 3, ad. 1.

[92] Loughlin, "Similarities and Differences," 51.

[93] Robert C. Roberts' criticism of the Thomistic categorization of the passions as physicalistic is based on the failure to appreciate this distinction in Aquinas' treatment: "Thomas Aquinas on the Morality of Emotions," *History of Philosophy Quarterly* 9 (1992): 287–305.

[94] For instance, the pleasure experienced at the attainment of a sensed good ("delight") is distinct from the pleasure experienced at the attainment of an intellectual good ("joy"). *ST*, I–II, Q. 31, a. 3.

[95] "Aquinas on Emotion," 166.

[96] See Thomas Dixon, *From Passions to Emotions: The Creation of a Secular Psychological Category* (Cambridge: Cambridge University Press, 2003).

[97] "Morality of Emotions," 287.

[98] *ST*, I–II, Q. 24, a. 1.

[99] "Morality of Emotions," 289.

[100] *De Veritate*, Q. 25, a. 1.

[101] Elizabeth Uffenheimer-Lippens, "Rationalized Passion and Passionate Rationality: Thomas Aquinas on the Relation between Reason and the Passions," *The Review of Metaphysics* 56 (2003): 525–558, 549.

[102] *De Veritate*, Q. 25, a. 4.

[103] "Morality of Emotions," 290.

[104] Mark D. Jordan, "Aquinas's Construction of a Moral Account of the Passions," *Freiburger Zeitschrift für Philosophie und Theologie* 33 (1986): 71–97, 95–96.

[105] *ST*, I–II, Q. 24, a. 1.

[106] Judith Barad, "Aquinas on the Role of Emotion in Moral Judgment and Activity," *The Thomist* 55 (1991): 397–413, 410. Cf. Craig Steven Titus, *Resilience and the Virtue of Fortitude: Aquinas in Dialogue with the Psychosocial Sciences*, (Washington, D.C.: The Catholic University of America Press, 2006), 109–127.

[107] G.J. McAleer, "The Politics of the Flesh: Rahner and Aquinas on *Concupiscentia*," *Modern Theology* 15 (1999): 355–365.

[108] Uffenheimer-Lippens, "Rationalized Passion," 548–49.

[109] "Emotions — A View through the Brain," *Neuroscience and the Person: Scientific Perspectives on Divine Action*, (Berkeley: Center for Theology and the Natural Sciences, 1999), 101–118. For a more technical discussion of his work, c.f., Joseph E. LeDoux, "Cognitive — Emotional Interactions: Listen to the Brain," *Cognitive Neuroscience of Emotion*, (New York: Oxford University Press, 2000), 129–155.

[110] Elizabeth A. Phelps, "The Human Amygdala and Awareness: Interactions Between Emotion and Cognition," in *The Cognitive Neurosciences*,, vol. 3, ed. Michael S. Gazzaniga, (Cambridge: The MIT Press, 2004), 1008. C.f., S. M. Schaefer, D. C. Jackson, R. J. Davidson, D. Y. Kimberg, and S. L. Thompson-Schill, "Modulation of Amygdalar Activity by the Conscious Regulation of Negative Emotion," *Journal of Cognitive Neuroscience* 14 (2002): 913–921.

[111] Klein, *The Science of Happiness*, 64.

[112] F. Engert and T. Bonhoeffer, "Dendritic Spine Changes Associated with Hippocampal Long-Tterm Synaptic Plasticity," *Nature* 399 (1999): 66–70.

[113] Dr. Baxter and his associates observed that obsessive-compulsive patients whose feelings and symptoms improved with behavior therapy also displayed changes in the prefrontal cortex, the thalamus, and the caudate nucleus at the end of treatment. L. R. Baxter Jr., et al., "Caudate Glucose Metabolic Rate Changes with Both Drug and Behavior Therapy for Obsessive-Ccompulsive Disorder," *Archives of General Psychiatry* 49 (1992): 681–89.

[114] Jaak Panksepp, *Affective Neuroscience: The Foundation of Human and Animal Emotions*, (NY: Oxford University Press, 1998), 301: "When the mushrooming of the cortex *opened* up the relatively *closed* circuits of our old mammalian and reptilian brains, we started to entertain alternatives of our own rather than of nature's making. We can choose to enjoy fear. We can choose to make art out of our loneliness. . . . We can be warm or acerbic, supportive or sarcastic at will. Animals cannot. These are the options that the blossoming of the human cerebral mantle now offers for us."

[115] *ST*, I–II, Q. 35, a. 2.

[116] Ibid., ad. 3.

[117] Ibid., a. 3, ad. 1.

[118] Ibid., a. 4.

[119] Paul J. Glenn, *A Tour of the Summa* (Rockford, IL: Tan Books and Publishers, 1978), 128–129.

[120] *ST*, I, Q. 14, a. 10.

[121] Ibid., I–II, Q. 36, a. 1.

[122] Ibid., a. 2.

[123] Ibid., a. 3 and 4.

[124] Giuseppe Barzaghi, "La *passio tristitiae* secondo S. Tommaso. Un esempio di analisi realista," *Sacra Doctrina* 36 (1991): 56–71, 63.

[125] *ST*, I–II, Q. 37, a. 1.

[126] Stephen Loughlin, "*Tristitia et Dolor*: Does Aquinas Have a Robust Understanding of Depression?" *Nova et Vetera* 3 (2005): 761–84, 767.

[127] *ST*, I–II, Q. 37, a. 2.

[128] Ibid.

[129] AllPsych ONLINE, http://allpsych.com/disorders/mood/majordepression.html, last accessed 2/20/2006.

[130] *ST*, I–II, Q. 37, a. 3.

[131] Ibid.

[132] *ST*, I–II, Q. 39, a. 1.

[133] Ibid., a. 2.

[134] Ibid., a. 2, ad. 2 and 3.

[135] Ibid., a. 4.

[136] Ibid., a. 3.

[137] Nonetheless, if it is an accurate perception of and response to an real evil, even impotent sorrow is preferable to a complete lack of sorrow, as it implies at least some perfection of the relevant human capacities.

[138] *ST*, I–II, Q. 39, a. 3, ad. 3.

[139] *ST*, I–II, Q. 38, a. 1.

[140] Barzaghi, "La passio tristitiae," 66.

[141] *ST*, I–II, Q. 38, a. 2.

[142] *ST*, I–II, Q. 38, a. 2, ad. 1.

[143] *ST*, I–II, Q. 38, a. 5.

[144] Ibid., ad. 1.

[145] Loughlin, "*Tristitia et Dolor*", 776.

[146] *ST*, I–II, Q. 3, a. 5.

[147] Ibid., Q. 38, a. 4.

[148] Ibid., ad. 1.

[149] Ibid., a. 4.

[150] *ST*, I, Q. 80, a. 2.

[151] Granted, it is conceivable that such intense emotional responses to weather patterns and the like have a chemical basis, but since, as has been shown, the physiology of depression is not understood, there is no hard evidence to support this theory.

[152] Loughlin, "*Tristitia et Dolor*", 782.

[153] Drost, "Intentionality," 449.

[154] Ibid.

[155] Breggin, *Antidepressant Fact Book*, 9.

[156] *ST*, I–II, Q. 39, a. 4.

[157] William E. May, *An Introduction to Moral Theology* (Huntington: Our Sunday Visitor Publishing, 2003), 23.

[158] For an account of the historical and conceptual relationship between systematic denials of morality, moral systems not based on human fulfillment, and moral systems based on human fulfillment, C.f. MacIntyre, *After Virtue.*

[159] Eberhard Schockenhoff, *Natural Law & Human Dignity: Universal Ethics in an Historical World*, trans. Brian McNeil (Washington: Catholic University of America Press, 2003), 200.

[160] Really, most of the discussions of antidepressant drugs are at this level; the use of a drug is good if it reduces symptoms and has few side-effects.

[161] *Natural Law and Practical Reason: A Thomist View of Moral Autonomy*, trans. Gerald Malsbary (NY: Fordham University Press, 2000), esp. 351–410.

[162] Ibid., 361.

[163] It has always seemed to me that Grisez is right on this point, and that Hume's "is-ought" dilemma from the *Treatise on Human Nature* (III) is a logical correlate to exposition of the natural law in the *Summa* (I–II, Q. 91, a. 3).

[164] *Humanae Vitae*, no. 7. All English translations of pontifical documents can be accessed at http://www.vatican.va/phone_en.html.

[165] Ibid., no. 14.

[166] Ibid., no. 9.

[167] *Humanae Vitae*, no. 9.

[168] No. 50, as quoted by *Humanae Vitae*, no. 9.

[169] Ibid., nos. 10, 12.

[170] Ibid., no. 13.

[171] Ibid., no. 31.

[172] *Familiaris consortio*, no. 11.

[173] I am aware of the fact that the papal teaching on contraception is much debated, even among Catholics, with regard to both its authority and its cogency. However, to engage in this debate would be too lengthy an excursus, and so I will assume here that the official documents quoted make a valid argument and arrive at true conclusions.

[174] *Gaudium et Spes*, no. 27.

[175] Although I do not agree with much of the work of Grisez, Boyle, and Finnis, I believe that this limited incorporation of some of their insight will compliment our present argument, harmonize with the traditional model of virtue and human flourishing, and bring an important voice in moral theology into the discussion. I do not believe this incorporation adds any radically new claim to what has gone before in chapter two and the first half of chapter three, and consequently I do not believe it will add any increased burden of proof to my overall argument.

[176] Germain Grisez, *The Way of the Lord Jesus* vol. I (Chicago: Franciscan Herald Press, 1983), 123.

[177] Germain Grisez, Joseph Boyle, and John Finnis, "Practical Principles, Moral Truth, and Ultimate Ends," *The American Journal of Jurisprudence* 32 (1987): 99–151, 108.

[178] Again, it is certainly conceivable that biochemical levels may be related to de-

pression in some or all cases, but any tangible evidence attempting to support such a theory is inconclusive.

[179] Kramer, *Listening to Prozac*, 254.

[180] Ibid., 255.

[181] Ibid., 259.

[182] Ibid., 254.

[183] Ibid., 17.

[184] C.f. Aquinas, *ScG*, II, 122; *ST*, I–II, Q. 75, a. 1; John Gallagher, "The Principle of Totality: Man's Stewardship of His Body," in *Moral Theology Today: Certitudes and Doubts*, ed. Donald G. McCarthy (St. Louis: Pope John Center, 1984), 217–242; Benedict Ashley and Kevin O'Rourke, *Health Care Ethics: A Theological Analysis* (Washington: Georgetown University Press, 1997), 219; Germain Grisez, *The Way of the Lord Jesus*, vol. 2. *Living a Christian Life* (Quincy: Franciscan Press, 1993), 542; William E. May, *Catholic Bioethics and the Gift of Human Life* (Huntington: Our Sunday Visitor Publishing, 2000), 308.

[185] We have defined depression as a generalized sorrow directed at life/the world in general. Whether this originates from sorrow to a specific perceived evil that is then extended universally (as Aquinas suggests), or from an original misunderstanding about the world itself is not relevant here. The point is that the world is perceived/experience/judged in a negative light, with depression as the result.

[186] "Aspirin for the Mind? Some Ethical Worries about Psychopharmacology," in *Enhancing Human Traits: Ethical and Social Implications*, ed. Erik Parens, (Washington, D.C.: Georgetown University Press), 135–50, 143.

[187] Ibid.

[188] *The New Yorker*, 69. (November 8, 1993): 92.

[189] If it the immateriality or existence of the soul be denied, (which in some cases it certainly is), then the discipline of psychology would do well to rename itself and define itself as a species of biology rather than the study of the soul.

[190] C.f., Nancy Murphy, *Bodies and Souls, or Spirited Bodies?* (NY: Cambridge University Press, 2006), 67.

[191] In other words, those traits which make antidepressants distinctive. For example, we will not talk about the placebo effects of the drugs.

[192] *ST*, I–II, Q. 39, a. 3.

[193] Fyodor Dostoevsky, *Crime and Punishment*, trans. Richard Pevear and Larissa Volokhonsky, (NY: Alfred A. Knopf, 1993).

[194] William Shakespeare, *MacBeth* , (NY: Cambridge University Press, 1997).

[195] "Pursued by Happiness and Beaten Senseless: Prozac and the American Dream," *The Hastings Center Report* 30 (2000): 7–12.

[196] Elliot, *Better Than Well*, 157.

[197] *Man's Search for Meaning: An Introduction to Logotherapy* (NY: Simon & Schuster, 1984), 108.

[198] *ST*, I–II, Q. 39, a. 1.

[199] *The Problem of Pain*, (NY: HarperCollins, 2001), 124.

[200] *Charter for Healthcare Workers*, 1995, no. 102. In no. 100, the charter includes under the category of psycho-pharmaceuticals those medicines used to overcome depression.

[201] Glenmullen, *Prozac Backlash*, 233–271.

[202] Ibid., 253.

[203] Ibid., 271.

[204] This does not mean that alcohol can never be abused in a way similar to anti-depressant abuse. Certainly, someone who regularly "drowns his sorrow" is purposefully disjointing his emotions from cognition in a morally impermissible manner.

[205] As quoted by Conrad W. Baars, preface to Anna A. Terruwe and Conrad W. Baarsk, *Psychic Wholeness and Healing: Using ALL the Powers of the Human Psyche* (NY: Alba House, 1981), ix.

[206] Unlike Shawn D. Floyd, Terruwe and Baars do not distinguish in terminology between the "passion" of sense and of rationality. "Passion" is simply translated as "emotion."

[207] *Psychic Wholeness*, 11.

[208] Ibid.

[209] Conrad W. Baars, *Feeling & and Healing Your Emotions* (Gainesville: Bridge-Logos, 2003), 19.

[210] *Psychic Wholeness*, 14.

[211] *ST*, I–II, Q. 74, a. 1, ad 1.

[212] *Psychic Wholeness*, 26.

[213] Ibid.

[214] Ibid., 42.

[215] Ibid., 38.

[216] Ibid., 39.

[217] Ibid., 64.

[218] Ibid., 65.

[219] Ibid., 66, 139–141.

[220] Ibid., 67–71.

[221] Ibid., 71–75. Note that, as in the Thomistic discussion, the psychiatric states often produce physical correlations, but that these two are never equated.

[222] Ibid., 76–79.

[223] Ibid., 79–85.

[224] Ibid., 97.

[225] Ibid., 90.

[226] Ibid., 97.

[227] Ibid., 93–95.

[228] Ibid., 100.

[229] Ibid., 110–11.

[230] Ibid., 127–130.

[231] Ibid., 127.

[232] Conrad W. Baars, *Born Only Once: The Miracle of Affirmation* (Quincy, IL: Franciscan Press, 2001), 22–23.

[233] *Faith, Hope, Love* (San Francisco: Ignatius Press, 1997), 174–176.

[234] Anna A. Terruwe and Conrad W. Baars, *Healing the Unaffirmed: Recognizing Emotional Deprivation Disorder*, eds. Suzanne M. Baars and Bonnie N. Shayne Staten Island: St. Paul's, 2002), 8.

[235] Ibid., 10–12.

[236] Ibid., 20–28.

[237] Ibid., 32, 34.

[238] Ibid., 36–38.

[239] Ibid., 22–23.

[240] Ibid., 76–77.

[241] Ibid., 78–79

[242] Ibid., 94–103.

[243] Ibid., 118.

[244] Ibid., 106–111.

[245] Ibid., 120.

[246] *Psychic Wholeness*, 130.

[247] *Healing the Unaffirmed*, 35.

[248] Ibid., 82.

[249] *God, Suffering, & Belief*, (Nashville: Abingdon, 1977), 120.

[250] Alasdair C. MacIntyre, *Difficulties in Christian Belief* (NY: Philosophical Library, 1960), 36.

[251] On the concept of actualizing the power to not choose the good, c.f., Jacques Maritain, *God and the Permission of Evil*, trans. Joseph W. Evans (Milwaukee: The Bruce Publishing Company, 1966).

[252] Lewis, *Problem of Pain*, 24. On the practical impossibility of constant divine interventions for the sake of precluding all evil, c.f. David Basinger, "Evil as Evidence Against God's Existence: Some Clarifications," *Modern Schoolman* 58 (1980–1981): 175–84, and Michael Peterson, "Recent Work on the Problem of Evil," *American Philosophical Quarterly* 20 (1983): 321–40.

[253] Thomas makes the distinction between the "evil which is penalty," of which God is the author, and the "evil which is fault" of which God is not the author. *ST* I, Q. 49, a. 2.

[254] Philadelphia: (Fortress Press, 1975), 9–32.

[255] Ibid., 134.

[256] Cf. Arthur C. McGill's theology of a "needy" God: *Suffering: A Test of Theological Method* (Philadelphia: The Westminster Press, 1982).

[257] *Suffering*, 114.

[258] *Difficulties*, 22.

[259] Jn 9:3; Lk 13:4–5.

[260] John Paul II, *Salvici Doloris*, no. 10, italics in the original.

[261] John Paul II, *Salvici Doloris*, no. 26.

[262] Lewis, *Problem*, 90–91.

[263] Ibid., 94.

[264] (NY: (Penguin Books, 2004), 99.

[265] *Problem*, 96.

[266] Ibid., 97–98.

[267] *Suffering*, 30–32.

[268] Ibid., 109–19.

[269] Ibid., 113.

[270] Lewis, *Suffering*, 100–101.

[271] *Evil and the God of Love* (London: The Macmillan Press, 1977), 258.

[272] *Confessions*, Book 8, Chapter 11, Para. 25. Trans. J. G. Pilkington (NY: Liveright Publishing Corporation, 1942).

[273] Ibid., 8, 7, 16.

[274] Trans. E. Allison Peers (Garden City: Image Books, 1961), 170.

[275] Book II, Chapter 5; trans. E. Allison Peers (NY: Doubleday, 1990), 101–02.

[276] Ibid.

[277] In Teresa's words, "Comfort must come to them from above, for earthly things are of no value any more." Teresa of Avila, *Interior Castle*, trans. E. Allison Peers (Garden City: Image Books), 132.

[278] *Suffering*, 148.

[279] (Garden City: Image Books, 1977), 10–11.

[280] Ibid., 9.

[281] *Salvici Doloris*, 16.

[282] Sheen, *Life*, 9.

[283] John Paul II, *Salvici*, no. 26.

[284] Ibid., no. 19.

[285] No.15.

[286] Ibid., no. 107.

[287] Ibid., no. 44.

[288] Ibid., no. 106.

[289] John Paul II, *Salvici Doloris*, no. 26.

BIBLIOGRAPHY

American Medical Association. *Essential Guide to Depression*. New York: Pocket Books, 1998.

American Psychiatric Association. *Diagnostic and Statistical Manual of Mental Disorders*. Vol. 4. Washington, DC: American Psychiatric Association, 2000.

Appleton, William S. *The New Antidepressants and Antianxieties: What You Need to Know about Zoloft, Paxil, Wellbutrin, Effexor, Clon azepam, Ambien, and More*. New York: Plume, 2004.

Ashley, Benedict, and Kevin O'Rourke. *Health Care Ethics: A Theological Analysis*. Washington: Georgetown University Press, 1997.

Augustine of Hippo. *Confessions*. Translated by J. G. Pilkington. New York: Liveright Publishing Corporation, 1942.

Axelrod, J., R. Whitby, and G. Hertting. "Effects of Psychotropic Drugs on the Uptake of Tritiated Noradrenaline by Tissues." *Science* 133 (1961): 383–84.

Baars, Conrad. *Born Only Once: The Miracle of Affirmation*. Quincy, IL: Franciscan Press, 2001.

———. *Feeling and Healing Your Emotions*. Gainesville : Bridge-Logos, 2003.

Barad, Judith. "Aquinas on the Role of Emotion in Moral Judgment and Activity." *The Thomist* 55 (1991): 397–413.

Barondes, Samuel H. *Better Than Prozac: Creating the Next Generation of Psychiatric Drugs*. New York: Oxford University Press, 2005.

Barzaghi, Giuseppe. "La passio tristitiae secondo S. Tommaso. Un esempio di analisi realista." *Sacra Doctrina* 36 (1991): 56–71.

Basinger, David. "Evil as Evidence against God's Existence: Some Clarifications." *Modern Schoolman* 58 (1980–1981): 175–84.

Baxter, L. R. Jr ., et al. "Caudate Glucose Metabolic Rate Changes with Both Drug and Behavior Therapy for Obsessive-Compulsive Disorder." *Archives of General Psychiatry* 49 (1992): 681–89.

Breggin, R. Peter. *Toxic Psychiatry: Why Therapy, Empathy, and Love Must Replace the Drugs, Electroshock, and Biochemical Theories of the "New Psychiatry."* New York: St. Martin's Press, 1991.

————. *The Antidepressant Fact Book: What Your Doctor Won't Tell You About Prozac, Zoloft, Paxil, Celexa, and Luvox.* Cambridge: Perseus Publishing, 2001.

Braun, Stephen. *The Science of Happiness: Unlocking the Mysteries of Mood.* New York: John Wiley and Sons, 2000.

Burkle, Howard. *God, Suffering, and Belief.* Nashville: Abingdon, 1997.

Casey, Nell, ed. *Unholy Ghost: Writers on Depression.* New York: Perennial, 2002.

Connor, T. J., and B. E. Leonard. "Biological Markers of Depression." *In Antidepressants: Past, Present, and Future*, edited by Sheldon H. Preskorn, John P. Geighner, Christina Y. Stanga, and Ruth Ross. New York: Springer, 2004.

Coyle, Joseph T., and Ronald S. Duman. "Finding the Intracellular Signaling Pathways Affected by Mood Disorder Treatments." *Neuron* 38 (2003):157–60.

Dixon, Thomas. *From Passions to Emotions: The Creation of a Secular Psychological Category.* Cambridge: Cambridge University Press, 2003.

Dostoevsky, Fyodor. *Crime and Punishment.* Translated by Reichard Pevear and Larissa Volokhonsky. New York: Alfred A. Knopf, 1993.

Drost, Mark P. "Intentionality in Aquinas' Theory of Emotions." *International Philosophical Quarterly* 31 (1991): 449–60.

Elliot, Carl. "Pursued by Happiness and Beaten Senseless: Prozac and the American Dream." *The Hastings Center Report* 30 (2000): 7–12.

————. *Better Than Well: American Science Meets the American Dream.* New York: W. W. Norton and Company, 2003.

Engert, F., and T. Bonhoeffer. "Dendritic Spine Changes Associated with Hippocampal Long-Term Synaptic Plasticity." *Nature* 399 (1999): 66–70.

Fink, Max. *Convulsive Therapy: Theory and Practice.* New York: Raven, 1973.

Fisher, Seymour, and Roger P. Greenberg. "Mood-Mending Medicines: Probing Drug, Psychotherapy, and Placebo Solutions." In *From Placebo to Panacea: Putting Psychiatric Drugs to the Test,* edited by Seymour Fisher and Roger P. Greenberg. New York: John Wiley and Sons, Inc., 1997.

Floyd, Shawn D. "Aquinas on Emotion: A Response to Some Recent Interpretations." *History of Philosophy Quarterly* 15 (1998): 161–75.

Frankl, Viktor. *Man's Search for Meaning: An Introduction to Logotherapy.* New York: Simon and Schuster, 1984.

Freedman, Carol. "Aspirin for the Mind? Some Ethical Worries about Psychopharmacology." In *Enhancing Human Traits: Ethical and Social Implications,* edited by Erik Parens, 135–50. Washington, DC: Georgetown University Press.

Gallagher, John. "The Principle of Totality: Man's Stewardship of His Body." In *Moral Theology Today: Certitudes and Doubts,* edited by Donald G. McCarthy. St. Louis: Pope John Center, 1984.

Glenmullen, Joseph. *Prozac Backlash: Overcoming the Dangers of Prozac, Zoloft, Paxil, and Other Antidepressants with Safe, Effective Alternatives.* New York: Simon and Schuster, 2000.

Glenn, Paul J. *A Tour of the Summa.* Rockford, IL: Tan Books and Publishers, 1978.

Greene, Graham. *The End of the Affair.* New York: Penguin Books, 2004.

Greenberg, Paul E., Ronald C. Kessler, Tara L. Nells, Stan N. Finkelstein, and Erst R. Berndt. "Depression in the Workplace: An Economic Perspective." In *Selective Serotonin Re-uptake Inhibitors* Second Edition, edited by J. P. Feighner and W. F. Boyer, 327–63. Chichester: John Wiley and Sons, 1996.

Grisez, Germain. *The Way of the Lord Jesus.* Vol. 1. Chicago: Franciscan Herald Press, 1983

———. *The Way of the Lord Jesus.* Vol. 2, Living a Christian Life. Quincy: Franciscan Press, 1993.

Grisez, Germain, Joseph Boyle, and John Finnis. "Practical Principles, Moral Truth, and Ultimate Ends." *The American Journal of Jurisprudence* 32 (1987): 99–151.

Harak, G. Simon. *Virtuous Passions: The Formation of Christian Character.* Mahwah: Paulist Press, 1993.

Harmer, Catherine J., Simon A. Hill, Matthew J. Taylor, Philip J. Cowen, Guy M. Goodwin. "Toward a Neuropsychological Theory of Antidepressant Drug Action: Increase in Positive Emotional Bias after Potentiation of Norepinephrine Activity." *The American Journal of Psychiatry* 160 (2003): 990–92.

Healy, David. *The Antidepressant Era.* Cambridge: Harvard University Press, 1997.

———. *Let Them Eat Prozac: The Unhealthy Relationship between the Pharmaceutical Industry and Depression.* New York: New York University Press, 2004.

Hewitt, John P., Michael R. Fraser, and Leslie Beth Berger. "Is It Me or Is It Prozac? Antidepressants and the Construction of Self." In *Pathology and the Postmodern: Mental Illness as Discourse and Experience,* edited by Dwight Fee. London: Sage Publications 2000.

Hick, John. *Evil and the God of Love.* London: The Macmillan Press, 1977.

Hurst, W. D. "Biochemical and Physiological Processes in Brain Function and Drug Actions." In *Antidepressants: Past, Present, and Future,* edited by Sheldon H. Preskorn, John P. Geighner, Christina Y. Stanga, and Ruth Ross. New York: Springer, 2004.

John of the Cross. *Dark Night of the Soul.* Translated by E. Allison Peers. New York: Doubleday , 1990.

Jordan, Mark D. "Aquinas's Construction of a Moral Account of the Passions." *Freiburger Zeitschrift für Philosophie und Theologie* 33 (1986): 71–97.

Karp, David A. *Is It Me or My Meds? Living with Antidepressants.* Cambridge: Harvard University Press, 2006.

King, Peter. "Aquinas on the Passions." In *Thomas Aquinas: Contemporary Philosophical Perspectives,* edited by Brian Davies. New York: Oxford University Press, 2002.

Klein, Stefan. *The Science of Happiness: How Our Brains Make Us Happy—And What We Can Do to Get Happier.* Translated by Stephen Lehmann. New York: Marlowe and Company, 2006.

Knutson, Brian, et al. "Selective Alteration of Personality and Social Behavior by Serotonergic Intervention." *The American Journal of Psychiatry* 155 (1998): 373–79.

Knuuttila, Simo. *Emotions in Ancient and Medieval Philosophy.* Oxford: Clarendon Press, 2004.

Kramer, Peter D. *Listening to Prozac.* New York: Viking, 1993.

LeDoux, Joseph E. "Emotions—A View through the Brain." *Neuroscience and the Person: Scientific Perspectives on Divine Action.* Berkeley: Center for Theology and the Natural Sciences, 1999.

———. "Cognitive—Emotional Interactions: Listen to the Brain." *Cognitive Neuroscience of Emotion.* New York: Oxford University Press, 2000.

Lewis, C. S. *The Problem of Pain.* New York: HarperCollins, 2001.

Loughlin, Stephen. "Similarities and Differences between Human and Animal Emotion in Aquinas's Thought." *The Thomist* 65 (2001): 45–65.
——. "Tristitia et Dolor: Does Aquinas Have a Robust Understanding of Depression?" *Nova et Vetera* 3 (2005): 761–84.

Lynch, Terry. *Beyond Prozac: Healing Mental Suffering without Drugs.* Dublin: Marino Books, 2001.

MacIntyre, Alasdair. *Difficulties in Christian Belief.* New York: Philosophical Library, 1960.

——. *After Virtue.* Notre Dame, IN: University of Notre Dame Press, 1981.

Maritain, Jacques. *God and the Permission of Evil.* Translated by Joseph W. Evens. Milwaukee: The Bruce Publishing Company, 1966.

Maj, Mario, and Norman Sartorious. *Depressive Disorders.* 2nd. ed. West Sussex: John Wiley and Sons, 2002.

May, William E. *Catholic Bioethics and the Gift of Human Life.* Huntington: Our Sunday Visitor Publishing, 2000.

——. *An Introduction to Moral Theology.* Huntington : Our Sunday Visitor Publishing, 2003.

McAleer, G. J. "The Politics of the Flesh: Rahner and Aquinas on Concupiscentia." *Modern Theology* 15 (1999): 355–65.

McGill, Arthur C. *Suffering: A Test of Theological Method.* Philadelphia: The Westminster Press, 1982.

Mitchell, E. Siobahn. *Antidepressants.* Philadelphia: Chelsea House Publishers, 2004.

Morrison, James. *Straight Talk about Your Mental Health.* New York: The Guilford Press, 2002.

Murphy, Claudia Eisen. "Aquinas on Our Responsibility for Our Emotions." *Medieval Philosophy and Theology* 8 (1999): 163–205.

Murphy, Nancy. *Bodies and Souls, or Spirited Bodies?* New York: Cambridge University Press, 2006.

National Institute of Mental Health. *The Numbers Count: Mental Disorders in America.* http://www.nimh.nih.gov/publicat/numbers.cfm. Date last accessed 3/13/2007.

Nestler, Eric J., Michel Barrot, Jalph J. DiLeone, Amelia J. Eisch, Stephen J. Gold, and Lisa M. Monteggia. "Neurobiology of Depression." *Neuron* 28 (2002): 13–25.

Norden, Michael J. *Beyond Prozac: Brain-Toxic Lifestyles, Natural Antidotes, and New Generation Antidepressants.* New York: Regan Books, 1996.

Panksepp, Jaak. *Affective Neuroscience: The Foundation of Human and Animal Emotions.* New York: Oxford University Press, 1998.

Peterson, Michael. "Recent Work on the Problem of Evil." *American Philosophical Quarterly* 20 (1983):321–40.

Phelps, Elizabeth A. "The Human Amygdala and Awareness: Interactions between Emotion and Cognition." In *The Cognitive Neurosciences.* Vol. 3., edited by Michael S. Gazzaniga. Cambridge: The MIT Press, 2004.

Pieper, Josef. *Faith, Hope, Love.* San Francisco: Ignatius Press, 1997.

Pierce, Robert A., Michael P. Nochols, and Joyce R. Dubrin. *Emotional Expression in Psychotherapy.* New York: Gardiner Press. 1983.

President's Council on Bioethics. *Beyond Therapy: Biotechnology and the Pursuit of Happiness.* http://www.bioethics.gov/reports/beyond therapy/beyond_therapy_final_webcorrected.pdf. Date last accessed 3/16/2007

Preskorn, S. H., and R. Ross. "Overview of Currently Available Antidepressants." In *Antidepressants: Past, Present, and Future,* edited by Sheldon H. Preskorn, John P. Geighner, Christina Y. Stanga, and Ruth Ross. New York: Springer, 2004.

Rhonheimer, Martin. *Natural Law and Practical Reason: A Thomist View of Moral Autonomy.* Translated by Gerald Malsbary. New York: Fordham University Press, 2000.

Roberts, C. Robert. "Thomas Aquinas on the Morality of Emotions." *History of Philosophy Quarterly* 9 (1992): 287–305.

Sapolsky, Robert M. "Will We Still Be Sad Fifty Years from Now?" In *The Next Fifty Years: Science in the First Half of the Twenty-First Century*, edited by John Brockman, 105–13. New York: Vintage Books, 2002.

Schaefer, S. M., D. C. Jackson, R. J. Davidson, D. Y. Kimberg, and S. L. Thompson-Schill. "Modulation of Amygdalar Activity by the Conscious Regulation of Negative Emotion." *Journal of Cognitive Neuroscience* 14 (2002): 913–21.

Schockenhoff, Eberhard. *Natural Law and Human Dignity: Universal Ethics in an Historical World.* Translated by Brian McNeil. Washington: Catholic University of America Press, 2003.

Shakespeare, William. *MacBeth.* NY: Cambridge University Press, 1997.

Sheen, Fulton J. *Life of Christ.* Garden City: Image Books, 1977.

Soelle, Dorothee. *Suffering.* Philadelphia: Fortress Press, 1975.

Sorabji, Richard. *Emotions and Peace of Mind: From Stoic Agitation to Christian Temptation.* Oxford: Oxford University Press, 2000.

Sweeney, Gladys M. *Introduction to Human Nature in Its Wholeness: A Roman Catholic Perspective,* edited by Daniel N. Robinson, Gladys M. Sweeney, and Richard Gill. Washington, DC: Catholic University of America Press, 2006.

Teresa of Avila. *Interior Caste.* Translated by E. Allison Peers. Garden City: Image Books, 1961.

Terruwe, Anna A., and Conrad W. Baars. *Psychic Wholeness and Healing: Using ALL the Powers of the Human Psyche.* New York: Alba House, 1981.

———. *Healing the Unaffirmed: Recognizing Emotional Deprivation Disorder.* Edited by Suzanne M. Baars and Bonnie N. Shayne. Staten Island: St. Paul's 2002.

Titus, Craig Stephen. *Resilience and the Virtue of Fortitude: Aquinas in Dialogue with the Psychosocial Sciences.* Washington, DC: The Catholic University of America Press, 2006.

Trullas, Ramon. "Functional NMDA Antagonists: A New Class of Antidepressant Agents." In *Antidepressants: New Pharmacological Strategies,* edited by Phil Skolnick, 103–24. Totowa: Humana Press, 1997.

Turkington, Carol, and Eliot F. Kaplan. *Making the Antidepressant Decision: How to Choose the Right Treatment Option for You or Your Loved One.* Chicago: Contemporary Books, 2001.

Uffenheimer-Lippens, Elizabeth. "Rationalized Passion and Passionate Rationality: Thomas Aquinas on the Relation between Reason and the Passions." *The Review of Metaphysics* 56 (2003): 525–58.

Walach, Harold, and Irving Kirsch. "Herbal Treatments and Antidepressant Medication." In *Science and Pseudoscience in Clinical Psychology*, edited by Scott O. Lilienfeld, Steven Jay Lynn, Jeffrey M. Lohr. New York: The Guilford Press, 2003.